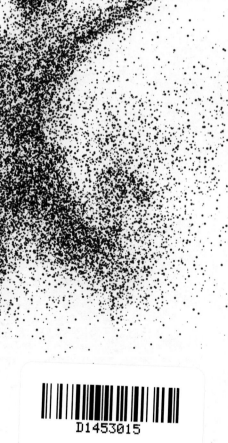

D1453015

As Jesus left the house, he was followed
by two blind men crying out,
"Mercy, Son of David! Mercy on us!"

When Jesus got home,
the blind men went in with him.

Jesus said to them,
"Do you really believe I can do this?"

They said, "Why, yes, Master!"
He touched their eyes and said,
"Become what you believe."

It happened.
They saw.

~Matthew 9:27–30 MSG~

BELIEVE
BECOME
BE

BECOMING THE MAN
GOD BELIEVES YOU CAN BE

ROBERT NOLAND

iDisciple®

Believe Become Be

Copyright © 2019 Robert Noland.

All rights reserved. No part of this book may be reproduced in any form or by any electronic or mechanical means, including storage and retrieval systems, photocopy, recording, scanning, or other, without permission in writing from the publisher, except by a reviewer who may quote brief passages in a review. Copying this book is unlawful and unethical.

Published by Giving Publishing, 2555 Northwinds Parkway, Alpharetta, GA 30009. In association with the literary agency of The WTA Group, Franklin, TN.

Unless otherwise noted, Scripture quotations are taken from the Holy Bible, New Living Translation (NLT). Copyright © 1996, 2004, 2007, 2013, 2015 by Tyndale House Foundation. Used by permission of Tyndale House Publishers, Inc., Carol Stream, Illinois 60188. All rights reserved.

Scripture quotations marked MSG are from *The Message*. Copyright © 1993, 1994, 1995, 1996, 2000, 2001, 2002. Used by permission of NavPress Publishing Group.

Scripture quotations marked NLV are taken from the *New Life Version,* copyright © 1969 and 2003. Used by permission of Barbour Publishing, Inc., Uhrichsville, Ohio 44683. All rights reserved.

Scripture quotations marked NIV are from THE HOLY BIBLE, NEW INTERNATIONAL VERSION®, NIV® Copyright © 1973, 1978, 1984, 2011 by Biblica, Inc.® Used by permission. All rights reserved worldwide.

Scripture quotations marked NKJV are taken from the New King James Version®. Copyright © 1982 by Thomas Nelson. Used by permission. All rights reserved.

Scripture quotations marked TLB are from The Living Bible copyright © 1971 by Tyndale House Foundation. Used by permission of Tyndale House Publishers Inc., Carol Stream, Illinois 60188. All rights reserved. The Living Bible, TLB, and The Living Bible logo are registered trademarks of Tyndale House Publishers.

Scripture quotations marked NCV are taken from the New Century Version®. Copyright © 2005 by Thomas Nelson. Used by permission. All rights reserved.

ISBN: 978-1-7331380-2-4

Written by Robert Noland
Edited by Christy Distler
Design by Amy Balamut

CONTENTS

Believe

- Consider to be true or honest

- Accept the word or evidence of

- Accept something as true, genuine, or real ideals we believe

- Have a firm or wholehearted religious conviction or persuasion to regard the existence of God as a fact

- Have a firm conviction as to the goodness, efficacy, or ability of something

- Hold an opinion[1]

Become

- Come into existence

- Come to be

- Undergo change or development

- Be suitable to

- To be

- To happen to[2]

Be

- Equal in meaning: have the same connotation
- Have identity with: to constitute the same idea or object
- Constitute the same class as
- Have a specified qualification or characterization
- Belong to the class of
- Have an objective existence: have reality or actuality
- Have, maintain, or occupy a place, situation, or position
- Remain unmolested, undisturbed, or uninterrupted
- Take place[3]

A Word from Robert Before You Begin

Concise Content & Short Chapters

After having been involved with men's ministry for a decade and talking to guys around the country, I have intentionally structured this book so you can have "quick victories" in being able to throw down a chapter in a half hour or less. Consume, take it in, process it, pray, and move forward. How this book is put together is very much on-purpose for busy men.

We

Throughout the majority of this book I use the word "we." The words "you" or "I" are used on occasion only for certain emphasis. This is a "we" book because *you are not alone.* You have a heavenly Father, so therefore you have a bunch of brothers. Listen, I'm just as much of a sinner and struggler as you, so everything in this book pertains to me too. So when I say *we,* I mean *we.* I want to invite you out of cultural isolation and into Christ's influence. Together, let's *be we,* okay?

Scripture

Isaiah 55:11 states, *"It is the same with my word. I send it out, and it always produces fruit. It will accomplish all I want it to, and it will prosper everywhere I send it."* In this book, I use a lot of Scripture, *like a lot.* The reason is although I am an author, my words will fail and fall away, but God's Word stands and produces life. Please read every Scripture in these pages, even if you *think* you know it. The biblical context is vitally important for a full understanding of the teaching. When I repeat a passage, that too is intentional, because we will use it in a different context. All Scripture is italicized to clearly separate my words from God's. His Words will change your life; mine won't.

Christ Follower

Unfortunately in our western culture, the word "Christian" has come to have various connotations, many of which no longer describe disciples of Jesus Christ. In these pages, I use the term "Christ follower" to describe a man who has decided to truly follow Jesus today. I want to separate that man who by grace is living in obedience to become the man God believes Him to be.

Small Groups

A great way to walk through this book is with a couple of other guys on a weekly basis. Read a chapter. Get together. Talk about it. Pray on it. Being honest and processing this teaching with other men will give new life to these spiritual topics.

Dads

If you're a dad of a pre-teen-and-up son, go through the book with him. Use this as a "men's manual" to talk about some of the tough topics of manhood that your son is now or will be facing very soon. You can adapt the material and discussions to his level.

Introduction

But I Need Something More!

Having placed the majority of my kingdom efforts over the past decade in men's ministry, there is one major frustration I see in my own life. But I have also heard this same struggle resonate with men everywhere, regardless of how long a Christ follower, age, race, income, locale, or any other cultural marker. Here it is:

We choose to follow Christ.

We want to please our heavenly Father.

We desire to live in the power of the Holy Spirit.

We read and become familiar with the beliefs of the Bible and agree with them.

Yet we struggle on a daily basis to convert what we believe into actually being God's man. In short, we desperately desire through our *beliefs* to *become* the man we envision God made us to *be*.

That is not to say that we do not change or make progress over time. But there always seems to be some thing, or things, issues, and problems, that plague and nag us, creating a deep desire to someday rise above to conquer and defeat them.

I have a good friend who calls his goal image of who he wants to become, his phantom— some alter ego that makes the right decisions and says the right things and has the right attitude and motives. We all understand what he is talking about.

But we can take great comfort and be encouraged by the apostle Paul when he so transparently shared in Romans 7:15–20:

Yes. I'm full of myself—after all, I've spent a long time in sin's prison. What I don't understand about myself is that I decide one way, but then I act another, doing things I absolutely despise. So if I can't be trusted to figure out what is best for myself and then do it, it becomes obvious that God's command is necessary.

But I need something more! For if I know the law but still can't keep it, and if the power of sin within me keeps sabotaging my best intentions, I obviously need help! I realize that I don't have what it takes. I can will it, but I can't do it. I decide to do good, but I don't really do it; I decide not to do bad, but then I do it anyway. My decisions, such as they are, don't result in actions. Something has gone wrong deep within me and gets the better of me every time. (MSG)

Man! When we read his words, we say, "Yeah, Paul. Thanks, sir. I totally get how you feel. Me too."

So I decided to title this book after one of our greatest frustrations this side of Heaven, but also the goal of our lives as men who follow Christ: *Believe. Become. Be.* We want to encourage one another to *believe* God, to cooperate with His Holy Spirit to *become* what He ultimately wants us to *be* as we transform into the image of Christ.

We don't ever say, "I want to *do* peace." We say, "I want to *be* at peace." I want to *do* faithful? No, I want to *be* faithful. I want to *do* self-control? No, I want to *be* self-controlled. Why? Because *do* is an action in which we start and stop, while *be* is a state we are in, or a reality, an "actuality," like the dictionary definition states a few pages back.

I want you to know I did not write this book because I am an expert on anything. I wrote it because I want to honestly inspire and encourage men to know you are not alone in your spiritual struggles, as you desire to be obedient to Christ.

Whether you are a dad or not, we all know our deep innate desire as men for a father to believe in us. We all want that sense of knowing, feeling, and sensing the pride of a father in who we have become and what we can accomplish.

Far too many of us battle with the belief that our heavenly Father *believes* in *us*. He is sovereign and omniscient, so we understand He knows our hearts and minds. But to walk through life with the knowledge that our Abba Father, as Jesus called Him, deeply loves us, desires to bless us, and believes we can be everything He designed, created, and gifted us to be is an extraordinary and miraculous gift. I cannot find anything in Scripture that says we cannot believe and embrace that truth in our lives.

So with that premise in our hearts, let's dive into some tough topics—some areas that can frustrate us all—and together find some answers in the Answer, a way in the Way, truth in the Truth, and life in the Life. Let's talk about how to become a man of purity, truth, and righteousness, to be a man after God's heart in Jesus' name for His glory.

Part One

Believing,
Becoming,
Being
a Man of Purity

Chapter One

New Mind, New Motive, New Mission

For if a man belongs to Christ,
he is a new person.
The old life is gone.
New life has begun.
—*2 Corinthians 5:17 NLV*

In my forty years of ministry, I have taken on many different roles in the church and in para-church organizations. I have been a pastor of a church and a janitor of a church. The biggest difference is when you are a janitor, cleaning up the messes is way easier.

But in every role in each setting, what I have seen proven time and again is that the real difference made in anyone's circumstances, whether Heaven or Hell on earth, whether deliverance or decadence, is that the outcome is not about what we do with the situation, but rather what we allow

Jesus to do in the situation. Do we ignore Him or invite Him in when He knocks on the door? And He will most certainly knock. He will show up, but He will never force His way into the room.

For all the issues and crises that create our problems, Christ alone is the Solution and He alone is the Prescription for our pain. Will we allow Him to reach into the recesses of our wretchedness and redeem every last drop of our humanity? To become, as we move from believing to being?

I have a dear friend and mentor who has been a counselor for decades. Often, after hearing a man's problems, he typically asks, "So what do you really want? Will you do the work to change your life? Are you willing to pay the personal price of obedience?" He draws a line in the sand early on because he has seen again and again that so many men want solutions without sacrifice. He calls this mindset "slot machine faith," as in "I want to put in a few quarters and hit the jackpot"— little effort, little energy, little investment, but big payoff.

Yet real life just does not work that way as much as we can wish it did. Following Christ certainly does not work that way. Yes, His grace is *amazing* and always *available,* but only total surrender is what gets us to His finish line.

To follow Christ, the only way to get to see the checkered flag is to first wave the white flag.

As we dive into many of the difficult and sometimes dark issues of manhood, if you are not willing to put in some work just as my counselor friend challenges his clients to do, then the back cover of this book is going to look just like the front cover. Just reading something will never change your life. The ultimate proof is that people read the Bible all the time without actually experiencing any spiritual change. There are atheists who know and can quote Scripture. The question is always what will we do with the content, the information we take in.

But what if deciding to *believe* in God's only Son to *become* His man ultimately brings you to *be* whom you have always hoped and wanted to *be*?

If you are unfamiliar with Christianity and not yet sure about this "Jesus stuff," I want to challenge you to stay open as you read and keep pressing through. Give Him a shot. What do you have to lose? What do you have to gain besides everything? What if you find some real answers to your life's questions and issues?

Application is Arrival

Application of what you read is the key. If everyone who read the Bible actually applied God's principles to experience real life change, we'd be living in a vastly different world today.

We know our world is full of if/then statements, and the Bible is no exception, with God offering us hundreds of these possibilities for our lives.

But don't just listen to God's word. You must do what it says. Otherwise, you are only fooling yourselves. For if you listen to the word and don't obey, it is like glancing at your face in a mirror. You see yourself, walk away, and forget what you look like. But if you look carefully into the perfect law that sets you free, and if you do what it says and don't forget what you heard, then God will bless you for doing it. (James 1:22–25)

How does God promise to bless you here? Look at and listen to His Word. Do what it says and do not forget it as you live. Believe to become to be.

All religions or belief systems assume you are ignorant of their ways when you first believe. You are then taught their "truth," or major pillars. When you understand those points, you become enlightened or move into revelation of knowledge in the beliefs. Most of the world's religious systems teach that if you go from ignorance (not knowing) to knowledge (knowing), you have arrived. You understand and embrace the teaching therefore you are changed. Understanding is arrival.

But *does* arrival come with understanding? Is that *really* true?

When do you *know* someone loves you? When they tell you they understand the concept of love? When they speak the words *I love you?* No. You believe someone loves you when you experience actual acts and affirmations of love from the person.

In our culture, another example of knowledge versus application is the university degree. When ten people apply for a job with credentials that state they have moved from ignorance to knowledge in a specific expertise, how does a prospective employer know who can best apply what they have learned even after hearing them answer specific questions? Well, the reality is they can't until there is a track record of actual work for evidence. Just because someone "looks good on paper" does not mean he/she is the best candidate.

Think about your own journey. How did you get *good* at what you do? And how many of us end up doing something vastly different from our college degree or other credentials state because we got actual experience at another career? We can only become great at what we apply.

On the subject of parenting, which couple most often appears to know exactly what to do in every single circumstance concerning a child? Those couples with *no* kids. Because the knowledge of all they *plan* to apply someday sounds amazing. The strategy on paper is to raise perfect children, but living with a two-year-old will quickly change all that when application becomes necessary. Plans have no variables, while life is full of them.

Our sense of getting good at anything comes through commitment coupled with experience. For years we have heard it takes ten thousand hours dedicated to a skill to become an expert. Connecting this concept to us as men who follow Christ, we grow by commitment coupled with experience. When you talk to a man who has put in ten thousand hours of walking with God intimately, you won't just know it; you will also feel it. There is only one way to gain such experience. Put in the time. Expend the energy. Do the work. Knowledge to application. Believe to become to be.

Show-and-Tell Experience

Jesus changed everything upon His arrival, including what a true faith or belief system asks of its followers. He wanted His disciples to not only understand but to also apply. He wanted belief to be a bridge to being. Not a classroom lecture hall with a whiteboard, but a technical school warehouse full of real tools that you use. When we follow Jesus, arrival comes at application, not simply understanding. He didn't just teach and then go off and leave His disciples. They did not arrive until they had lived life with Him. This indicates a lifestyle far past mere Sunday morning *attendance* once a week. This requires day-to-day *experience* with Him.

Where in the Bible do we see Jesus teaching and do not find Him before or after—or both—being involved in actual ministry with real people? He could have easily walked into the temple every day and just quoted from the Torah and then ended with an awesome closing prayer. But He did so much more. The temple was a part of His life, but not *all* of His life. The application of the Father's will was His only goal from baptism to ascension.

Jesus never practiced tell-and-go, but show-and-tell. He was consistently inviting His followers inside what He was doing. "Oh, you want to walk on water? Okay, step out of the boat into the waves." "You have no food but need to feed thousands of people? Go get me that little boy's lunch. I've got something to show you." "If you want to get rid of these particular demons, you're going to have to join me in prayer and fasting before you rebuke them." Jesus was continually fueling, training, and preparing His followers for life *after* the resurrection.

"I tell you the truth, anyone who believes in me will do the same works I have done, and even greater works, because I am going to be with the Father." (John 14:12)

See it? Application. From believing in Him to being His body. Jesus told His followers how much and how well they would learn to apply belief after He left. He knew they were becoming His bride.

Putting Faith into Practice

The church you attend today is a result of those early Christians *applying* Jesus' teaching and *duplicating* His actions, not simply believing in something or someone. What if Peter had decided he had been enlightened with Jesus' teaching and that was enough? No, he believed so he became. He transformed through the Holy Spirit's power coupled with his obedience. That's how the same guy who stayed silent and denied Jesus three times the night of the trials became God's mouthpiece who led thousands to salvation in the very same Savior. When you trace Peter's life from the denial of Christ to the preaching at Pentecost, anyone would have to admit that something major happened to this guy! He had become! He *be!*

So let's sum up: We are to believe, so we can become.

Now personalize it: I am to believe, so I can become.

Peter and the other disciples were not crucified upside down for just believing in a cause. They were nailed upside down for their actions—for what they were being. They just could not stop being Jesus to the world, so people had to kill them to stop them.

This incredible passage shows us our roots in Christ:

How much more do I need to say? It would take too long to recount the stories of the faith of Gideon, Barak, Samson, Jephthah, David, Samuel, and all the prophets. By faith these people overthrew kingdoms, ruled with justice, and received what God had promised them. They shut the mouths of lions, quenched the flames of fire, and escaped death by the edge of the sword. Their weakness was turned to strength. They became strong in battle and put whole armies to flight. Women received their loved ones back again from death. But others were tortured, refusing to turn from God in order to be set free. They placed their hope in a better life after the resurrection. Some were jeered at, and their backs were cut open with whips. Others were chained in prisons. Some died by stoning, some were sawed in half, and others were killed with the sword. Some went about wearing skins of sheep and goats, destitute and oppressed and mistreated. They were too good for this world, wandering over deserts and mountains, hiding in caves and holes in the ground. All these people earned a good reputation because of their faith, yet none of them received all that God had promised. For God had something better in mind for us, so that they would not reach perfection without us. (Hebrews 11:32–40)

Jesus never said, "I am a trained God-Man. Please, kids, don't try this at home." No, He told us to practice His truths at home, at work, with our friends, *as we go* through life.

"Therefore everyone who puts these words of mine into practice is like a wise man who built his house on the rock. The rain came down, the streams arose, and the winds blew and

beat against that house; yet it did not fall because it had its foundation on the rock." (Matthew 7:24–25 NIV)

If you put something "into practice," you take the concept from belief to being. A doctor in practice is administering care to patients—being a doctor. A lawyer in practice is administering legal expertise to clients—being a lawyer. A Christ follower in practice is administering Jesus to the world—being His body.

Jesus, undeterred, went right ahead and gave his charge: "God authorized and commanded me to commission you: Go out and train everyone you meet, far and near, in this way of life, marking them by baptism in the threefold name: Father, Son, and Holy Spirit. Then instruct them in the practice of all I have commanded you. I'll be with you as you do this, day after day after day, right up to the end of the age." (Matthew 28:18–20 MSG)

Who is the "you" in that last promise statement? It was them! It is us! You. Me. All His followers. Jesus was communicating a lifestyle, which the disciples carried on and lived out. This is now our calling. The reason we are on the earth today and the only activity that will matter for eternity.

So, in light of all we have discussed thus far, how can we tell what we really believe? Do we really believe that which we *don't* do? Do we really believe that which we *won't* do?

In a Christian book or message of any kind, anytime you stress any sort of doing, action, or practice, depending on a reader's biblical worldview, we can fall too far on the works side or too far on the grace side. A lot of Christians feel they must prove their worth through their work. But there are also many Christians who feel grace covers us to the point that obedience to truth is not that important, that grace offers some sort of free pass to poor decisions.

But a thorough study of the New Testament shows us a clear balance of works (obedience) and grace. Obedience through action is crucial to our walk with Christ, yet His grace is also vital in covering the fact that we are all sinners incapable of perfection who need His mercy on a daily basis. No matter where you fall on the grace/works scale, I pray we all find a better and stronger balance by the end of our time together.

And just for proper perspective for us all, let's remember Jesus' words in John 15:5:

"Yes, I am the vine; you are the branches. Those who remain in me, and I in them, will produce much fruit. For apart from me you can do nothing."

There is a strong chance that you are reading this book because you are a man who follows Christ and your goal is life change. But maybe you are not yet a believer in Jesus Christ and are looking for answers and seeking truth. Maybe a friend or family member gave you this book. Regardless, your reading this book is not an accident, but rather a well-planned opportunity for you. No matter where you are coming from, stay open and pray for truth as you read.

If Christ really is the Truth, Life, and Way He declares to be in John 14:6, then He will reveal Himself to you in the pages of this book as we talk about Him and His teaching. If He is not, He won't. But I am banking He will. He is amazing at that. Years ago, I walked through this process from not believing to believing and then still today being on the journey of becoming to being. I wasn't raised in a Christian home and didn't even set foot in a church or hear about Jesus until I was twelve. The reality of the gospel did not sink in until I was nineteen. He showed me who He was and is—and who He is to me personally. He will do the same for you too.

If we were sitting together right now after talking through these topics, praying together before moving on would be a great way to wrap up, but this is as close as we are going to get for now, so . . .

"Heavenly Father, thank You that You sent Your Son, Jesus Christ, to make it possible for us to believe and to also have the privilege to be Your adopted sons. Thank You that Your Spirit gives us the tools to put faith into action. Thank You that the challenge of living in purity, truth, and righteousness is completely possible because of Your life, Your death, and Your resurrection. Help us to stay open to You throughout these pages to see, hear, and know Your truth because You are Truth. Please give us Your hope, strength, and courage to believe, to become, and to be Your followers, Your sons, Your body to the world. In Jesus' name, amen."

Chapter Two

Grace, Not Grief
Conviction, Not Condemnation

Remember that your bodies are created
with the same dignity as the Master's body.
You wouldn't take the Master's body
off to a whorehouse, would you?
I should hope not.
—1 Corinthians 6:15 MSG

Imagine for a moment living in the time when Jesus was in the midst of His ministry. You get word that He is about to start teaching on a nearby mountainside where there is lots of space and good natural acoustics for a crowd to gather and hear His message. You grab your buddies and start hiking up the hillside to find a good spot to see what all the fuss is about.

Seated within eye- and earshot of Him among the multitudes, you wait. Jesus walks up, leans against a rock, smiles at everyone, and begins. You are immediately amazed at how He makes you feel as if He is making eye contact only with you. He starts off talking about those who God blesses—the poor, the humble, mourners, ones who seek mercy and peace. You think to yourself, *This is different. Did he memorize this or is it impromptu? Oh well. Good stuff.*

He moves on to talk about salt and light as metaphors to our lives. *Deep, but I get it.* The next subjects up are the Law, why He came, and the importance of obedience. Then He addresses anger and the need for forgiveness. Jesus connects the idea of calling someone an idiot and cursing the person to the act of murder, as if to say you can commit murder in your mind and with your mouth by verbal character assassination. *Whoa. That's a tough one. I'll have to think on that a bit.*

But then the Lord says . . .

"You have heard the commandment that says, 'You must not commit adultery.'" (Matthew 5:27)

You smile and nod knowingly as He quotes the commandment, because not only do you know it by heart, but you're good on this one. Happily married now for several years, you have stayed clear of other women, especially *those* women. *I got this, Jesus. Next!*

But He continues and adds a surprise element you or anyone in the crowd did *not* see coming . . .

"But I say, anyone who even looks at a woman with lust has already committed adultery with her in his heart." (Matthew 5:28)

Oh, crap! Seriously? Did He really just say what I think He said? Thinking about a woman lustfully is the same as adultery? Hold up now! What? You do not dare turn to look at your friends, but you know they are just as shocked. Your mind is racing to connect the dots. *But only God can see and know my thoughts. . . . Oooooohhhhh . . . righhhhhhht. Never really considered that before.*

In one single sentence, Jesus redefined sexual sin, forever changing the paradigm of lust for everyone for all time. He put an omniscient God into the equation to change our perspective. Everyone knew the Law said adultery is forbidden, but they only applied that in the physical world, not the spiritual, mental, and emotional. Up to that day, the connotation was solely connected to the *act* of sex with someone other than your spouse.

Now the physical aspect is simply the completion of or the acting out of the thought that motivates and creates the actual sin. Think for a moment about how many men and women have committed adultery and then how many times they fantasized the act before finally engaging in it. What began in the mind was finally finished off with the body. Even someone who goes out for the first time and just picks up a random stranger has been playing with those thoughts for a long time.

So now Jesus said the sin has already been committed when the lustful thought occurs. To cover the base, I know some guys will think, *Well, if I've already sinned, I may as well finish it.* Let's just answer by saying that jumping from the frying pan into the fire is never a smart choice. The life-saving decision is to jump out of the pan and get away from the heat.

Let's go ahead and spell this concept out: You see a woman or the image of a woman and think to yourself, *Right now, this is what I would do with her.* The image, real or otherwise, has created a mental reality. This concept is also the idea behind Proverbs 23:7: *"For as he thinks in his heart, so is he"* (NKJV). In short, "What he thinks is what he is."

Of course, the context of Proverbs 23:7 is warning of eating a meal offered by a miser. He may tell you to eat your fill, but he will hold your actions against you if you eat his meal at all. But that is exactly what the Enemy does to us regarding lust. He tells us there is no harm in "eating our fill," but then will not let us live it down that we took him up on his offer!

I have heard men say, "But what I think about or fantasize, I would *never* actually do." I have talked with a lot of guys who had affairs who told themselves that very lie for years . . . until the Enemy gave them an opportunity. To be clear, I am not trying to make any man into Satan's victim, because we *always* have a choice in how we respond. Contrary to mythical belief, he cannot make us do anything. Even actual possession is through an invitation of some sort. However, the Enemy does have an extensive training program that he starts with young men as early as possible, and, like any sexual predator, he tells the guy to just keep it their little secret.

Impure Purity

For at least the past several decades, with the prevalence of the internet, the advanced indoctrination of sexual lust typically begins with the first taste of pornography. The end goal for the Enemy is to create an ongoing craving that leads out of the mind to the physical, meaning sex acts biblically defined as *any* sexual activity outside of marriage.

The training can lead to scarring people forever with heartache, shame, regret, guilt, insecurity, and feelings of worthlessness, along with physical manifestations such as abortions, STDs, divorces, severed families, lost careers, lost reputations, and on and on the list goes.

So if the training begins in the mind, doesn't it make total sense why Jesus would say, "anyone who even looks at a woman with lust"?

Consider this: When do we truly have victory over something? When we stop doing the activity? Or when that activity is no longer even a thought to us? An addict of any kind can sometimes make it through several days without a fix, but the reality is a fix is all he/she has thought about. Victory in our actions is the *final* step. Victory in our motives and thoughts opens the door to true freedom and deliverance.

Over the past decade in speaking to men at Christian events, when I say, "We're going to talk about purity," what 99 percent of the crowd hears is, "We're going to talk about sexual sin." Isn't it interesting how our culture has muddied and meddled with so many words to change their original connotation? Today in most circles, purity actually means impurity because we have come to see purity, particularly the biblical brand, as some kind of mythical elusive creature.

The reality we must face in the body of Christ is when we teach about purity today, we have to discuss all the hot-button topics such as lust, porn, and sexual addictions. Does anyone really *want* to discuss these issues? No. I know I certainly didn't. But we are at a crisis point, so now we actually have no choice but to address them head-on. To avoid these issues is sticking our heads in the sand.

Yet we must see how the Enemy has us up against the wall in this area, because we spend so much time now on all the things we need to *stop* that we struggle to take the time to discuss what we should *start*. If the Enemy has us constantly either fighting off temptation or living in guilt and shame, he has us right where he wants to keep us.

Regardless, we have to expand this discussion by understanding that biblical purity is so much deeper and broader than just sex. It is about our inner life, our thought life, and the deep recesses of our hearts, which is what Jesus was actually addressing. Sexual temptation is most definitely a *part* of that, but not *all* of that. Our actions are born from thoughts rooted in our minds and driven by the need in our souls. That is where we must start.

In Matthew 5 Jesus taught us that the sexual war is not waged below the belt, but above our eyebrows. We lose when the mind is turned from a battleground into a playground.

The Spirit Behind the Law

God always has a life principle behind every command-ment or law. His rules are never just for the sake of a rule or the goal of human domination. In Matthew 5:21–22, Jesus teaches the same principle with murder as He does with adultery. Both are main topics in two of the Ten Com-mandments, so this is an important connecting point. The spirit of the Law is not so much about murder as it is about respecting life that God created. Unforgiveness, judgment, and hatred are roadblocks to love and life. To so hate some-one's existence that we want the person dead is the ultimate judgment, and we were never intended to take such author-ity. The spirit of the Law is not so much about adultery as it is about respecting marriage and relationships. The obe-dience to the commandments begins and ends with being pure in your mind and heart.

The Law says do not commit murder. The spirit of the Law is not about death, but life. If you make a practice of respecting and appreciating life, you won't commit mur-der. The Law says do not commit adultery. The spirit of the Law is do not think about another woman other than your own wife. See the bigger picture? To be pure, to be holy as He is holy, is to focus on the one woman God gave you. The true concept is not about the *other* woman, but *the* woman.

The practical bottom line is if a tempting thought is stopped in the doorway to the mind, then the action will never get into our house and cause trouble.

To cover the base for single men: Applying the spirit of the Law when you are single can keep you from sexual sin and also prepare you for a holy and healthy marriage. No one can expect to allow their thoughts to run wild for years and then on the wedding day bring them all into the corral and expect them to stay in the barn forevermore.

I have talked with so many young single guys who say, "Well, when I get married, I'll be so in love and ready for a wife that lust won't be an issue anymore." (Another great lie in the training program of the Enemy.) If it is an issue now, it will be an issue then. Saying "I do" isn't going to flip that switch off. Those rationalizing ideas never come from God, only the Tempter because he knows you are being trained right now for your future. Surrendering and submitting your mind to God as if you are *already married* is the best decision you can make for your own life and health.

True purity is the absence of the motive or the thought that would motivate the wrong action. And this is the ultimate goal for us in every aspect of our lives, not just sexually. Remove the motive, which then kills the thought, which then prevents the action. This is not talking about perfection, not at all. But we have to biblically raise the bar and believe God can help us achieve ever-increasing purity in *any* area of life.

Let's say you and a couple of guys meet regularly for accountability and prayer. For most men who follow Christ, staying out of a situation where you might have sex with someone other than your wife is going to be fairly straightforward. You can tell each other where you were physically and geographically in the past week. You can give an account to each other regarding your whereabouts on any business trips. You can discuss any situations where you were around women in close contact. You have a good shot at success by accounting for yourself among brothers.

But does it not change everything to agree that our goal is to talk honestly and openly about our *thoughts?* Suddenly, it's not so much about our calendar anymore, or simply staying away from certain situations or women. It is no longer enough to just divulge my whereabouts and actions so you know I have not gotten into trouble. To maintain my purity, I now have to talk to you about my desires, attitude, thoughts, and even motives.

That mindset, gentlemen, is a game changer.

All the ways of a man are pure in his own eyes,
but the Lord weighs the thoughts of the heart.
(Proverbs 16:2 NLV)

Chapter Three

Treat the Source, Not the Symptoms

We fight with weapons that are different
from those the world uses.
Our weapons have power from God
that can destroy the enemy's strong places.
. . . We capture every thought
and make it give up and obey Christ.
—*2 Corinthians 10:4–5 NCV*

Maintaining biblical purity begins at its source—the mind. Jesus knew that then. Jesus knows that now. He was and is a Master at cutting through the symptoms and getting to the real root of the problem. When You are the Creator of all things, You can do that really well.

When the Law was given and stated "Do not commit murder" and "Do not commit adultery," those statements only attacked the symptoms, not the actual root. If you are at the place where you are telling yourself, *I can't murder this person* or *I can't commit adultery with her,* aren't you past the front door and already dangerously into the house?

So Jesus came to show us the root. Interesting that one of His names in Scripture is "The Root of Jesse." Of course that name has to do with genealogy and prophecy, but continually in situation after situation in Scripture He showed us the source of the problem with our sin, while also offering practical answers.

In the story where the woman was caught in adultery and brought before Jesus (Luke 8:1–11), one or more of the guys grabbing the rocks had to be her partners in crime. "Caught in adultery" never means you were by yourself. So when Jesus gave his two famous lines: "Let he that is without sin cast the first stone" and "Go and sin no more," no one there was going to stay out of sin again unless they first changed their minds about the direction of their lives. Even "go and sin no more" has to have a deeper meaning, namely, "Time to change your life, and here I am to help you."

I want to pause here to clarify a very important point. Having a thought is *not* a sin. That is the introduction of the temptation. How else is the Tempter going to tempt us? No one suddenly begins a physical act of sin without the idea being planted, entertained, and plotted out. Again, Jesus said "looks lustfully," meaning the thought was not rejected as a temptation but has moved on to reality as a sin.

When the thought enters our mind, we have a choice. Dismiss or do. Reject or invite in. If someone stands at your front door with a temptation, just because they are at your door does not mean you have sinned. No, the opportunity may be present, but you have not yet engaged. You know that sin could happen if you open the door, so you either do not answer or tell the person to go away. If you go to the door and invite them in, that is taking part. The opportunity to sin is not a sin. The introduction of a thought is not a sin until it is invited in and entertained.

The Why Behind the What

In our culture today, we are notorious for treating symptoms, not the root cause. We work to stop behavior while ignoring the mind and heart driving the actions. Often if the problem has been created by a lifestyle that society has decided to now condone, then addressing someone's root problem is deemed intolerant. In the celebrity world, *rehab* has become a buzzword that actually has a mysterious cool factor attached. Any form of rehabilitation and counseling should be encouraged and applauded, but not glamorized.

But merely stopping a person from acting out does not change the heart. That approach will not uncover the unmet need that drove someone to bad behavior to begin with. By the time a person has acted on a thought, it is in its end form. The issue began in the mind, seeped into the heart and soul, and then eventually into the body and out through the person's actions. Particularly in the area of sexual sin, then the training begins to repeat the pattern.

If a guy in your small group has to call you every weekend to talk him out of going to meet up with some girl he met online, there is a battle that needs to be waged upstream.

Because he is constantly at the point of action, he is going to have to take a look at what is going on inside his mind and heart during the week *before* the weekend comes. So many folks end up back at square one because the root problem is never addressed.

From 2000 to 2009 I was the pastor of a small church plant. I never quit my "day job" of running a nonprofit ministry while pastoring "part time." During those years, I ended up ministering to just as many men outside our church as I did to those who were members. Word got out that I would listen to a guy no matter his issue or affiliation to try to help him. A lot of those men felt like they might be judged at their own churches, so they saw me in a sort of covert manner.

This was a typical scenario: A guy would call and nervously ask to meet. He would come in and stutter, him-haw, shuffle his feet, and wring his hands, doing all the nervous guy stuff we do. Typically, he would say something to the effect of, "I'm going to tell you something I've never told anyone. I'm really ashamed. Whatever you may think of me, that is likely about to change because this is really bad." Sometimes there was sweating, sometimes crying. Courage is hard to muster and often brings pain right before it gives birth.

Finally, like a man with a horribly nauseated soul, he throws up his issue. You name it and I've heard it. The issues and symptoms are endless, but the root cause is always the same— a heart problem. And that is true for every single one of us because we are all sinners.

My response was always the same. Still today when a guy opens up with me, I respond the same. "Okay, now that we've got out the symptom that's been eating you alive, I want you to know there is zero condemnation here. This is a place of grace. I am totally fine with you and what you just said. Your sin is no different to God than mine. In fact, I respect the fact that you would confess and desire to change. That's the hardest part—telling the secret. Now let's talk about *why* this has happened, or is happening, and *where* it may have come from. Let's try and get to the root of this issue." (Of course, if someone ever confessed a crime, that would change the agreement, but thank God that never occurred.)

But do you see it? It's not really about what the guy came in to confess. For him, that is the hard part. For me, that's the easy part. The real work for us *both* is figuring out the "why" now that the "what" is exposed. If a guy doesn't figure out the "why," he will likely find a new "what" or just keep struggling with his old one.

I have found that 99 percent of guys who are Christ followers who will walk in and confess a sin for the purpose of getting help have already beaten themselves up badly. In fact, if the emotional and spiritual bruises showed on them physically, the guy would be unrecognizable as a human. I heard a speaker years ago say that his accountability partner would tell him, "Put down your condemnation stick and stop beating yourself up so we can talk." Jesus rarely removes consequences, but He can stop our own condemnation immediately.

While we must speak truth and help each other deal with sin and its aftermath, we have to provide grace for each other to do the right thing, so we can get better, move on in health, and work toward the purity only Christ can provide. The reality is there are not enough pastors or counselors in the world to get to us all. So we have to decide to help each other. Be the church. Act like brothers. Show up for each other. Listen and love.

Trading Shame for Grace

When was the last time you hung your head before Jesus to confess a sin and suddenly found yourself in the middle of a Messianic beat-down? Doesn't happen. But when was the last time you confessed and heard His Spirit say, "You're forgiven. Now go and sin no more." (Yes, He says that to guys too.)

The beat-down comes from our own minds and the Enemy, so know that:

- Jesus disciplines, but He does not and will not deny you.

- Jesus offers grace, not grief.

- Jesus brings conviction, never condemnation.

- Conviction is God's call to repent, while condemnation is the Enemy's call to run.

Confession is not an end, but simply a beginning to the process of restoration. Throwing up the symptoms is the start to finding answers. Receiving and responding to discipline helps get us back in line with God.

Do not give up when you are punished by God. Be willing to take it, knowing that God is teaching you as a son. Is there a father who does not punish his son sometimes? If you are not punished as all sons are, it means that you are not a true son of God. You are not a part of His family and He is not your Father. Remember that our fathers on earth punished us. We had respect for them. How much more should we obey our Father in heaven and live? (Hebrews 12:7–9 NLV)

What in this world and beyond could possibly saturate our souls to the point of providing protection for us from our very own thoughts? The only Answer is the Holy Spirit of God provided by the sacrifice and security of Christ for an eternal relationship with our heavenly Father.

Who else can dive down into our motives and purify the very fiber of where our decisions are born? Who else can right our wrongs? I have personally found on countless occasions that I *cannot* possibly do this myself. I have tried a thousand times and I have failed a thousand times. But Jesus said that His Spirit will teach us all things and remind us of what we need to know.

But when the Father sends the Advocate as my representative—that is, the Holy Spirit—he will teach you everything and will remind you of everything I have told you. "I am leaving you with a gift—peace of mind and heart. And the peace I give is a gift the world cannot give. So don't be troubled or afraid." (John 14:26–27)

Let me be boldly honest with you. One of the greatest contradictions in life is someone who believes he has secured a home in Heaven, but lives helpless in Hell here. Regardless of whether or not you are a Christ follower or where you feel you are spiritually right now, regardless of how filthy you may feel or what you are guilty of, regardless of how shameful you are of your private thoughts or personal actions, God has a path to purity for you through Christ. (Yes, you.)

Jesus Christ can replace your shame with His grace. He can heal you, deliver you, and rescue you from the pit of Hell. That is His specialty. No one else can accomplish those things. He does it every day for those who call on His name. How do I know? How can I say that with such certainty? Because He has done so for me and continues to on a daily basis. Once His healing begins, the journey continues for life.

Those who are dominated by the sinful nature think about sinful things, but those who are controlled by the Holy Spirit think about things that please the Spirit. So letting your sinful nature control your mind leads to death. But letting the Spirit control your mind leads to life and peace. (Romans 8:5–6)

We must focus on the fact that there are real answers for our souls. If you are defeated by the way you have learned to live, Jesus can begin to change your mind. *Literally* change your mind, leading to "life and peace."

Chapter Four

The Lure of Lust

Hell has a voracious appetite,
and lust just never quits.
—Proverbs 27:20 MSG

Most men think of a lust problem as a sexual issue. But it is not. Lust is a heart problem. Lust is a symptom, not the root cause. For the nonbeliever, the root is rebellion. For the believer, the root is disobedience, because we have been saved out of rebellion and now know better.

The root issue is trying to meet a need on our own, rather than giving the authority to God and allowing Him to meet the need in His way. If you see lust as the only issue and you decide to work on not lusting, how successful is that method? How many men who love Jesus and are working hard on changing their lives by meeting with other Christian men spend time each week confessing the same sexual sin? We actually can think that the purpose is to just keep confessing while we have stopped believing that real change can happen.

As with any lust or addiction, sexual or otherwise, regardless of its object, the craving gets increasingly difficult to gratify so the demand is never satisfied. This is exactly why there are now millions, not thousands, of porn images online. The problem just keeps growing worse until it is no longer enough to simply look at digital images and fantasize. The desire leads to wanting to act out with someone. At this point for a man, the woman doesn't have to look like the made-up, photoshopped, and airbrushed girls in the photos or videos as long as they will do the things the guy has been imagining. (This is why most often a man's "mistress" is not as attractive as his spouse.)

Some very common things guys will tell themselves are, *Yeah, I spend several hours a week online, but I can quit whenever I want to; Well, I may be struggling with porn, but I would never have an affair; I've been flirting with this girl and we're getting dirty, but I would never actually do anything with her;* and *Okay, so I slept with her once, but I won't see her again. I'm done.* Unless something stops the downward spiral, the journey only has one destination, heading toward a bad ending.

If any of the scenarios so far have described you in any way, what should you do? First, you are going to have to be honest with yourself. You could slip farther down and go to the next step, and it could happen at any time. You could fall deeper. You are going to have to realize you are not the exception to the rule, so stop and get help. I know plenty of guys who wish to God every day they had taken steps before their lives went where they did. They wish they had listened to all the times God whispered in their ear to turn away from the addiction and turn to Him. If you know you are in trouble, listen and take brave action today.

Someone Somewhere Cares for Her Soul

Many years ago while the band I was in was leading worship at a student conference, I heard Christian author, communicator, and radio host Dawson McAllister define lust as "caring more for a woman's body than her soul." I have never forgotten his words. Such a great, practical, biblical definition.

There is a really funny thing I think most of us guys assume about Jesus as He was going about the countryside ministering and teaching: He was always around ugly women. He never had to deal with encountering a beautiful woman. He never had to handle a situation where a woman flirted with Him. He never had to hear men talk about the body of a woman who was serving their table. Nope, just a bunch of ugly women around Jesus. That is why He wouldn't or couldn't possibly understand what we deal with today in the modern age of the internet. . . . *Seriously?*

I'm sorry, but I just do not believe Mary Magdalene was not an attractive woman. The woman at the well had a track record of at least five men in her life. The "certain immoral woman" wiped Jesus feet with oil and her hair, while kissing his feet as she cried (Luke 7:36–50). Jesus talked with, ministered to, and hung out with women of all ages and stations of life. Therefore, He had to encounter some beautiful, attractive women. But in every single situation, we see nothing but respect and care from Him in a day when most men did not tend to behave that way because of how the male population at large viewed women.

I picture when any woman walked up to Jesus that He always looked into her soul by always looking into her eyes. And to use Dawson's definition, every woman knew, every time, that He, above all else, cared for their souls. When you read the conversations that Jesus had with women, He always talked about either her life or His Father. He did not talk about Himself, unless it was to make a reference about God. (I just cannot see Jesus grinning with one eyebrow up, bragging, "You should have seen the miracle I did the other day. You would have been amazed." Nope.)

As a result, women felt safe and did not feel threatened like they did with pretty much every other man in their life. The situation with the "certain immoral woman" proves this theory because she walked right in among a group of men, straight to Jesus, and began her very physical act of worship, fully focused only on Him.

When the Pharisee who had invited him saw this, he said to himself, "If this man were a prophet, he would know what kind of woman is touching him. She's a sinner!" (Luke 7:39)

But how did Jesus respond? He told the men a parable to teach them an important lesson and then honored the woman by recognizing her obedience to God.

Then Jesus said to the woman, "Your sins are forgiven." . . . And Jesus said to the woman, "Your faith has saved you; go in peace." (Luke 7:48, 50)

When the woman was caught in adultery, all the men who had stones in their hands cared nothing about her soul. *Before* Jesus walked up, they were focused on her body. *After* Jesus walked up, they were focused on themselves. Jesus focused only on her soul as He put the men in their place and then offered her grace.

Gentlemen, we cannot buy the Enemy's lie that we can *never* get to the point where we only care for women's souls. As Christ followers, that does not make any sense. Here's why:

While of course none of us are going to hit perfection this side of Heaven, is Jesus' life not the example and goal for us as men? Think about the women in your life whose souls you truly care for: Your mom. Your wife. Grandmother. Aunts. Sisters. Daughters. Daughters-in-law. Nieces. Granddaughters. Do you want your buddies to care about your wife or adult daughter's body or her soul? The "body" answer makes you want to fight, doesn't it? What should that tell us? We already know how to think in that manner, so we are just talking about expansion to the entire gender. Extending the same honor, chivalry, and courtesy to them all.

Do you see how if you truly began to care for *all* women's souls like you do for these special women in your life, that you don't have to focus so much on *not* lusting? You begin to focus on *doing the right thing,* rather than *not doing the wrong thing.* That is a very simple perspective change. We stay on offense, not so much on defense. Aren't you ready to *not* be on defense so much in this area?

The hooker on the street addicted to heroin has someone somewhere who cares for her soul. Even if only a grandmother who has not seen her in years but prays for her every night. The girl who posed for a "photographer" or "director" has someone somewhere who cares for her soul. Maybe only her little boy whom she is raising alone, the only reason she agreed to pose, because she needed the money to pay rent and buy food. Both of these young ladies are trying to meet temporary needs with solutions that could permanently devastate their future. But those details are never available because they are not sexy and they ruin the illusion.

Well, the world we live in today needs to see some men who follow Christ instead of their lusts, and who care for women's souls. The girl at the office. The woman down the street. The waitress. The barista. The convenience store clerk. Care for their souls. Jesus did. Jesus does. We can too. After all, we represent Him as His followers. Caring for the souls of *all* women because *each one* is special to God.

Supply & Demand

There is a major lie that the Enemy has done a great job of selling for generations. He tells men every day that—Jesus or no Jesus—no man can live without lust. But that is simply a lie from Hell. If he can convince you that you have no choice— that in fact, if you are a red-blooded, normal man, then you *should* lust—then he has a greater shot at robbing and destroying you. Maybe even eventually killing you (John 10:10).

Whether you are a teenager, a single man in his twenties, a thirty-something with a growing family, a middle-ager who has been married for decades, or a retiree with grandkids, lust can be dealt with. Temptations are *never* going to go away in this world. In fact, with the extreme sexual perversion of the culture, things will likely only get worse. But lust can be brought under the submission of Christ. Through Him, it can be controlled and stopped. Jesus proved that. He proved a man can live life, control Himself, and care about women's souls. Never forget while we can inspire and encourage one another by the lives we lead and the choices we make, Jesus is our ultimate Example and Goal.

If you just read that paragraph and you are thinking I'm crazy, well, which is more likely to help you live a pure life that honors Christ, your family, and women: to keep telling yourself the battle can never be won or *can* be won? But we all get to make our own choice and live with the outcome.

My own personal—not theological—opinion is that *one of the many reasons* Jesus never married was to show us the level of self-control and obedience that is available through a life surrendered to God's power. After all, He was all man as well as all God. That same power can impact the lust problem in your life. Temptation will still come but so can surrender to the One who cares for *all* souls, including yours.

I do not believe a man can put a stop to the demon of lust *without* the power of Christ, but I also do not believe a man can have any lasting change of *any* kind outside of the power of Christ.

Let's dive a little deeper here with a very serious question: Do women feel comfortable around you, or do you make them feel like they need to go through a purification rite after they've walked away? Women at work? At restaurants? At your workout facility? At church? If they all got together and discussed you, what would they say regarding you? Would they talk about how you check them out, look them up and down, or are flirty with suggestive comments? Or would they comment on what a gentleman you are and say they feel respected and on equal ground? They are attracted to your God because of how you speak and act around them?

Which guy are you? Which guy do you want to be? Well, the first guy you can be on your own. The second guy requires Christ to become. *Every* day.

A primary difference in these two guys is the first one makes it about himself and the second makes it about her. You see that? Women can spot that a mile away. Women know when a man is respecting them. Women are onto guys way more than we think. And the women who are naïve and do not get it? Unfortunately they usually end up hurt—by the first guy.

Allow me to address a thought I hear occasionally. Some guys think if the girls that pose for porn would just stop, then they would not have to be tempted to look. To put this in the terms of the business world, that is focusing on supply. Now let's turn the concept around.

What if the demand for these "models" ended? You think when the money dried up that these women would keep taking their clothes off? Do we really think they are doing it for the reasons that are fantasized about? Surely we know better than that. The porn industry is not about sex; it is about money. Gentlemen, just like with prostitution, when the money ain't there, the clothes stay on. Porn will not go away until the demand stops.

So choosing to live in purity is choking the demand out of *our* lives. One guy at a time. One soul at a time.

As we close this chapter, maybe you need to put this book down right now, grab your phone, and call a brother. Call your pastor. Maybe you need to get in your car and drive to a friend's house, look him in the eye, and ask for his help. (I once had a guy call me at 1:30 in the morning to tell me he was on his way to my house.) If you sense a conviction in your spirit to do something right now and do not act on it, then every time you say no to that voice, you sear your conscience and callous up a little more to God, until one day you will not give a rip what anyone says, including Him.

If this is not your issue or problem, that is awesome, so I want to ask you to do something a little strange, especially coming from a book. Would you stop right now and pray for *your* brothers, the guys in your circles, who need to take action to end their sin and addiction? What if right now your prayer could make the difference in one of your buddies getting help? Pray for them by name. Pray that God's Spirit would move men to action in the area of purity. Can you imagine if every guy who reads this chapter would pray for God to move in the hearts of the men in his circles?

I want to end with the words of King David, written after his sin with Bathsheba, after he was responsible for adultery, an unplanned pregnancy, and the murder of her husband, along with the lies his palace household witnessed. In his prayer are the hope and opportunity for us all, available from our heavenly Father.

God, be merciful to me because you are loving.
Because you are always ready to be merciful,
wipe out all my wrongs.
Wash away all my guilt and make me clean again.
I know about my wrongs, and I can't forget my sin.
You are the only one I have sinned against;
I have done what you say is wrong.
You are right when you speak and fair when you judge.
I was brought into this world in sin.
In sin my mother gave birth to me.
You want me to be completely truthful so teach me wisdom.
Take away my sin, and I will be clean.
Wash me, and I will be whiter than snow.
Make me hear sounds of joy and gladness;
let the bones you crushed be happy again.
Turn your face from my sins and wipe out all my guilt.
Create in me a pure heart, God,
and make my spirit right again.
Do not send me away from you
or take your Holy Spirit away from me.
Give me back the joy of your salvation.
Keep me strong by giving me a willing spirit.
Then I will teach your ways to those who do wrong,
and sinners will turn back to you.
God, save me from the guilt of murder, God of my salvation,

and I will sing about your goodness.
Lord, let me speak so I may praise you.
You are not pleased by sacrifices, or I would give them.
You don't want burnt offerings.
The sacrifice God wants is a broken spirit.
God, you will not reject a heart
that is broken and sorry for sin.
(Psalm 51:1–17 NCV)

Chapter Five

Fireplace & Wildfires

Can you build a fire in your lap and not burn your pants?
—Proverbs 6:27 MSG

Picture this: My wife and I are sitting at home one cold winter night and she asks, "Honey, would you get a fire going?" Wanting to be a good husband, I go to the garage and grab the gas can, get a lighter from the kitchen, and then stand over the rug in the middle of our living room floor, the one my wife loves that has the fringe along the edges.

I douse the rug with some gas and then carefully hold the lighter to the perfect line of fabric strands as I flick the igniter switch. The flame leaps out and the fringe catches fire, acting like fancy fuses leading to the thick cotton fabric. Like a good modern caveman, within minutes I have successfully created what my wife requested: a roaring fire in the living room.

She jumps up, screaming, "Are you crazy? What are you doing? Get the fire extinguisher!"

Confused by her reaction, I respond like any thoughtful husband, "Honey, what's wrong? I did exactly what you asked. I got a fire going."

Ridiculous scenario? Yes. That would be *crazy*. Responding with that solution to her request would just be wrong on every possible level. Creating a fire in that manner would confirm to my wife, once and for all, what I have given her plenty of reason over three-and-a-half-plus decades of marriage to wonder about me anyway.

The obvious problem would be my building a fire where a fire was never intended to be in my home—the right thing in the wrong place. Isn't it interesting that a fire being set just a few feet away from where it is supposed to be makes all the difference in right and wrong, good and bad, delight and devastation?

Fire is not bad. Fire in the wrong place is bad. Location is crucial.

Contrast my first fire story to this one: My wife makes the same request. I walk over to the metal box fitted into the wall and with the same lighter ignite the kindling I have tucked at the bottom of the logs stacked neatly inside. As the fire starts to catch, soon the logs begin to blaze up as well. The flames rise and the smoke goes up the chimney. As I pull the safety screen shut, my wife smiles. She is happy. The fire is beautiful. The fire is safe. We are warm and secure.

Many homes have this same appliance built into the wall, called a "fireplace." The literal meaning of the English word is "place of fire." (I'm joking, but couldn't we come up with something cooler than *fireplace?* That word just reeks of caveman-speak. I am grateful someone came up with *commode* and did not follow the same logic as fireplace.) In our homes, the fireplace is a designated and contained space where we can build a fire for both function and enjoyment.

The fireplace is also a great analogy for sex. Just like God created fire, He created sex. He designed sex for both function and enjoyment. But just like man has built the correct and safe place for fire in our homes, God created the correct and safe place for sex. Just like the builder puts a place in our homes for a fire to be made and contained for our ultimate satisfaction, God made a place for sex to be made and contained for our ultimate satisfaction.

Connecting the earlier fire analogy, isn't it interesting how sex, even just a few miles away, just a few houses down from where it is supposed to be, makes the difference in right and wrong, good and bad, delight and devastation?

Sex is not bad. Sex in the wrong place is bad. It's all about location.

Let's continue to build on this idea.

Avoiding Arson

Wildfires in California have become a devastatingly destructive force each year. Unfortunately, we have become accustomed to seeing the news clips of first responders driving through walls of flames on each side of the road. We have seen drone footage of planes dumping water through the smoke-filled skies onto the inferno below.

Thousands of acres are destroyed every year, entire towns burned to the ground, homes completely wiped out, and the worst part is that people's lives are scarred forever. The cause is sometimes from human error or something natural like a lightning strike. But all too often authorities discover a person has decided to intentionally start a fire just to witness destruction, driven out of some selfish desire or crazy whim.

When a man at any age, single or married, decides to engage in sex in the wrong location, he is starting a wildfire that will burn up lives, including his own. Whether a high school senior whose girlfriend informs him she is pregnant and getting an abortion, a college student who finds out he has a chronic or incurable STD, or a man who watches his affair destroy his family, tell me that does not feel like a wildfire raging, devastating people's lives forever. People get burned. People feel burned. Hearts and homes are destroyed forever. Sadly, these scenes play out many, many times every hour.

Every day, thousands of men watch their lives, their families, and all they have worked for go up in flames just about as fast as the orgasm occurred. And all too often the people hurt and affected by the sexual wildfire that he set are more likely to later begin setting fires of their own, born from the pain and the wounds created in them.

I am going to make a statement and you may think it sounds crazy. (You're getting used to this by now, aren't you? Stay with me.) Here we go:

Satan hates sex.

Why, you ask? Because:

- God created sex.

- God designed sex to be between one man and one woman in a committed and faithful marriage relationship.

- God ordained sex to be an act of worship to glorify Him as a reflection of ultimate intimacy.

- God provided sex as the creation method to populate the earth for the only species made in His image.

This is exactly why the Enemy's number-one attack against humankind is to get us to *misuse and abuse* God's gift. Therefore, sex is not dirty. The misuse of sex is actually what is filthy. Nothing God has created is bad in any way, for He is holy. Only the acts that corrupt and damage His creation are evil.

To connect our fire/sex analogies, God's gift of sex is the fireplace. Everywhere else is a wildfire. You can build an amazing roaring fire to enjoy for hours in a fireplace. A blazing fire built anywhere else is going to devastate and destroy. Sex is beautiful and holy for all those who choose to engage in His way in the right location—the marriage bed. Everywhere else, Satan uses sex to start wildfires born in Hell here on earth.

The Enemy wants to use a precious gift that God intended only for intimacy in marriage to rob, kill, and destroy God's children. He also wants to create the most fun for himself by watching us throw that gift back in the Creator's face, declaring we will use it how, when, where, and with whom we choose. The Enemy will then use sex as a source of shame, guilt, and regret for many years, sometimes a lifetime, far past when the act is over.

Sex in its God-given and God-ordained location is worship. In the marriage bed, the intensity of feelings, the love, and the pure, too-deep-for-words intimacy that happen between a husband (man) and wife (woman) who are truly in love and fully committed in marriage has been given as a gift to His sons and daughters. (Don't forget Song of Solomon is an entire book of the Bible.)

In marriage, this intimacy creates a triangle. God is at the pinnacle with the husband on one side and the wife on the other. As the couple lives out their relationship with God, each moves up their connecting side angle toward Him. This not only moves them closer to Him but also simultaneously draws the two closer together. The more marriage partners move toward God in agreement, the more unity will come.

With that understanding, doesn't it make sense why Satan hates marriage and sex so much, working to ruin and destroy both for *every* person on the planet? If it is a reflection of the depth of our relationship with God, if it has to do with a married couple's worship of God, if it brings us life to the full, then no wonder the Enemy makes sexual intimacy in marriage such a primary target of his wrath!

As the Scriptures say, "A man leaves his father and mother and is joined to his wife, and the two are united into one." This is a great mystery, but it is an illustration of the way Christ and the church are one. (Ephesians 5:31–32)

When we read the entire chapter of Ephesians 5 and get the correct understanding of mutual submission, marriage, and the God-ordained roles, we also start to understand why our post-Christian culture hates the concept of submission and rejects the biblical view of marriage.

This is exactly why Satan wants to get his claws into every young man and woman as soon as possible. If he can cause *anything* to disrupt, interrupt, or corrupt a young person's biblical understanding and soul imprint of love, sex, and marriage, he will. Early exposure to porn and overtly sexual images online create a false image in a child's mind as to what sex is actually about. And then if any other sexual activity or even abuse occurs, those can be open wounds for a lifetime. (If you are a young parent, I want to encourage you to get a plan for teaching your child the biblical view of sex, because I can promise you the Enemy already has one laid out. And you are likely the only person with the spiritual authority who can stop him.)

Over the last couple of decades, as my wife and I have met with couples, we've seen time and time again how one of the spouses in a Christian marriage was taught from a "biblical perspective" that sex is nasty and dirty, even in the marriage bed. That is just the Enemy coming in through a different door, while disguising himself as light.

From Pages to Pixels

If sex outside marriage is an arsonist's wildfire, then pornography is the accelerant in our culture. An arsonist not only wants to start a fire but spread the flames as far and wide and quickly as possible. As I have taught men over the past decade, I hear again and again how they have never heard biblical teaching regarding sex, sexual sin, and related issues. On many occasions, I have had men in their seventies and eighties come up to me with tears in their eyes, thanking me for teaching something they never thought they would hear. So next, we are going to delve more into where the misuse and abuse of sex leads from a spiritual and emotional sense.

First, I totally get why this is a really difficult subject to talk about, but if we are going to believe God created sex, then why can't we be the leaders in the culture teaching the proper worldview? The Scripture does not ignore the subject, so we shouldn't. Paul clearly addressed sexual sin that even much of the church today is now embracing.

When I was a kid growing up in the sixties and seventies (and if you are under thirty-five-ish, this is about to sound very foreign to you), the only way porn was even remotely and potentially accessible was by obtaining an actual magazine. For the most part, porn films were located in dives in very sketchy parts of metropolitan cities, and any sort of home video player had not even been invented yet.

So maybe you might find a magazine that someone had thrown out, or possibly some friend's dad or brother would have one. By the time you got old enough to actually walk into a store and purchase one of those magazines, you would have to go through the humiliation of asking the clerk for the title because they were kept out of view with brown paper covers on them. (You thirty-something guys—yep, I am totally serious.) I lived in a small town, so the chance that the store clerk didn't somehow know my dad or mom was slim. The risk was just not worth it. Even if someone subscribed to a magazine, the postman/woman knew *exactly* what was inside that brown paper cover with your address label attached. So everyone in town would soon know.

Bottom line: There were *lots* of personal and cultural obstacles in place to keep the majority of guys away from porn. If anyone would have told us back then that one day you could have a phone that you carry in your pocket that does not have a cord and you can pull up thousands of porn pictures and videos to watch on the screen, we would have, one, thought you were a delusional alien, and two, been hung up on a phone in your pocket with no cord *waaaaay* before we ever heard the word *porn*.

From that perspective, I find it really interesting how most typical families today would not even think of keeping a stack of porn magazines or videos lying on the coffee table or on the kitchen table, but they will put an unfiltered, unprotected iPad in the family room with twenty-four-hour access for their kids. We live in a day where the internet is no longer considered a luxury, but a necessity—food, water, shelter, online access.

Throughout my years in ministry, I have talked with a lot of addicts—alcohol, drugs, sex, relationships, and even food— but nothing seems to be as rampant and pervasive today as porn addiction. Sexual obsession meets socially acceptable access. An alcoholic has to go find a drink. A drug addict has to score. A sex addict has to find a partner. A food addict has to get to a drive-through. A porn addict just has to type in the six digits to unlock his phone. (I do not have a passcode on my phone, keep it lying face-up, and my wife can pick it up to scan through anytime she wants. That is not an invasion of privacy, but an installation of protection.)

Just like other addictions, the span of time between fixes becomes shorter and shorter. As the hooks are set deeper, time and energy is often spent anticipating and planning the next time. The hiding becomes more threatening and intense, while the frequency causes more carelessness. A vicious cycle of massive shame and momentary satisfaction starts to spin out of control.

I have no official data or reference to back up this claim, but over the past few years I have noticed a pattern in the news, of white males in their fifties and sixties who have no prior arrest record being charged for sex crimes. My theory is this: After being a normal career and family man for twenty-five to thirty years, they have two very dangerous dynamics in their lives—an obsession with or addiction to porn and boredom. So the images and videos are no longer enough. The next step is to find someone to act out the fantasies. And all too often because they cannot find a willing participant or do not want to risk a prostitute, they engage in a crime against a young woman or even a child.

Something a man never dreamed he would do ten years, even five years prior, becomes a rationalized option due to the transformation of the mind toward evil. Yes, just as the Holy Spirit can transform our minds to the ways of God, the mind can also be transformed by constant exposure to evil.

Porn is mental crack and emotional meth that wears away the spirit. Guys who would never consider doing drugs or getting drunk view porn differently from other vices. Having a phone, a tablet, and a laptop with a browser is normal, everyday fare. And porn is becoming more accepted each year in our culture. Celebrities make jokes about it during talk-show interviews, and what was once considered "soft porn" is now known as the TV or movie trailer, music video, or Instagram post.

If you could somehow know now that your ten-year-old son, grandson, nephew, or other loved one would be addicted to porn by the time he was twenty, what steps would you take to try to prevent that from happening? I am going to go out on a limb here and say it might be good to go ahead and formulate a plan now that begins with honest communication and education. So many parents say, "Well, I don't want to give him any ideas," when in reality, their child may have already been exposed and have bad info. And worse, he is already learning to keep it a secret.

Unfortunately, each year the stats show more and more girls are accessing and getting addicted to porn through several means. One, they are reading pornographic stories, with authors and filmmakers catering to that group as a niche. Two, they are looking at sites to find out what guys like so they can "keep their boyfriends happy." And three, some consume exactly in the same manner as guys.

To close this chapter, I want to share a passage where the prophet Isaiah was warning the people of God's judgment on their sexual immorality. Considering our culture today, if you think of porn as an idol, take a sober look at these words:

> *They, not I, are your inheritance.*
> *Do you think all this makes me happy?*
> *You have committed adultery on every high mountain.*
> *There you have worshiped idols*
> *and have been unfaithful to me.*
> *You have put pagan symbols on your doorposts*
> *and behind your doors.*
> *You have left me and climbed into bed*
> *with these detestable gods.*
> *You have committed yourselves to them.*
> *You love to look at their naked bodies.*
> *(Isaiah 57:6–8)*

Chapter Six

Vanquishing the Vicious Cycle

*Parts of me covertly rebel, and just when
I least expect it, they take charge.
I've tried everything and nothing helps.
I'm at the end of my rope.
Is there no one who can do anything for me?
Isn't that the real question?
The answer, thank God,
is that Jesus Christ can and does.*
—Romans 7:23–25 MSG

The typical cycle of porn is a guy feels alone, isolated, insecure, stressed, hurt, depressed, or disappointed. He wants somewhere "safe" to go that will make him feel better about himself. He turns to the females who will always take their clothes off, are always smiling and carefree, never say no, never have a headache or an emotional issue, and are always ready to go. They don't have to talk or require anything before sex.

No commitment. No expectations. No matter what time of day or night. They are just waiting there on the screen. Surfing begins, stimulation occurs, and momentary relief is experienced through masturbation.

But what happens immediately afterward, especially for the guy who professes to follow Christ? Within a few hours, maybe minutes, sometimes only seconds, condemnation floods in like a tsunami as a wave of shame swallows him up and holds him under until he cannot breathe.

I believe the Enemy gets two thrills when a man who follows Christ gives in to this temptation. First, there is the sin itself, which we will address more in a moment. But second, there is an opportunity to hurl accusations. He loves to whisper in the ear, beginning his assault, "You call yourself a Christian? What does your Jesus think about you now, huh? Big man of God you are!"

Feelings of self-hate and sadness pervade the soul. He continues his tirade two days later, a week later, a month later: "Hey, remember when you did that? That was filthy. You should be so ashamed. That's who you really are, you know. You're not the great Christian at all. What would everyone think if they knew about this?" You're sitting in church, singing a worship song or listening to a message, and here comes the voice: "Hey, remember last Tuesday? Who are you trying to fool? What a hypocrite." When you least expect it, when you are minding your own business, here he comes without warning like a schoolyard bully.

And then temptation rises up again and the cycle starts all over.

I think the Enemy has some of his biggest fun messing with men who follow Christ. What else does he have to look forward to? His fate is sealed and he has read the Book. What better for him to do than cripple and harass the very guys who are intended to obey and serve the King of Kings and Lord of Lords? The more we stand isolated in our little worlds, the more he is free to be the bully. But what if you and some friends circled up, stood together, put on the armor, drew the sword, and fought back together?

That Topic

This is as good a spot as any to address this taboo topic since you saw the word a few paragraphs back: *masturbation*. One of the many subjects our Western Christian culture has avoided so as not to be "offensive." But this subject is no longer off limits anywhere else in our society. Comedians, late-night TV talk-show hosts, artists, movie stars, and TV and film scripts all make the subject a joke or a brag quite often. Mainstream artists sing veiled songs about the subject disguised in lyrics like "loving yourself" or having a "party for one."

When I began to teach on this subject at men's retreats and events in 2009, I was not at all sure if I would get burned at the stake or blackballed. But what began to happen surprised me. Following the sessions, guys would line up, sometimes ten to fifteen deep, not to challenge or debate me, but to thank me for talking about the elephant in the room from a biblical standpoint.

The closest I ever came to having an issue was at one event where a man got up and made a dramatic point of storming out of the room. One of the pastors got up and followed him out. As the minister caught up with the man outside, the church member angrily protested, "Why are you allowing that guy to talk about these filthy subjects in our church? It's wrong!" The pastor looked him in the eye and said, "If you had any idea how many men I see every month in my office who are dying from the issues 'that guy' is addressing, you wouldn't be having a problem with this right now. We *have* to start talking about these things inside the church to help our men."

At the break between sessions, a man in his mid-thirties came up to me and said, "Hey, thank you for talking about these things with us. I also want to apologize for the man who walked out. He has way more issues than that one. He left out of conviction. I know because he's my dad." (Whoa. I had a feeling in that moment that the son was going to change some things generationally.)

If we will not talk about these tough topics and guys feel like they can't get help in the church, then who wins there? The Enemy. There are few issues where God is glorified by the church's silence.

Let's begin this most difficult topic by defining masturbation. (Yeah, I know you know, but there is a reason we need clarity.) Guys can tend to put masturbation in the category of "Things the Bible Doesn't Speak Directly About, Therefore We Obviously Are Able To Do Without Consequence." And by the way, if you look up masturbation in your Bible's concordance, you will find no references. But that is true with a *lot* of issues. So we have to take *all* Scripture in the area of sex and apply to the context.

Let's be simple and straightforward to define masturbation as "sex with yourself." If the physical act of sex is genital arousal for the goal of an orgasm, then masturbation is sex. Sex alone by yourself would qualify as "outside of marriage" or outside of the sanctity of "the marriage bed," so let's filter that thought through Paul's teaching on sex in 1 Corinthians 6. Eugene Peterson's modern take on this passage in The Message Bible is very compelling.

There's more to sex than mere skin on skin. Sex is as much spiritual mystery as physical fact. As written in Scripture, "The two become one." Since we want to become spiritually one with the Master, we must not pursue the kind of sex that avoids commitment and intimacy, leaving us more lonely than ever—the kind of sex that can never "become one." There is a sense in which sexual sins are different from all others. In sexual sin we violate the sacredness of our own bodies, these bodies that were made for God-given and God-modeled love, for "becoming one" with another. (16–18 MSG)

Here are some questions to consider as you think on these verses:

Is masturbation "mere skin on skin"? If so, then Paul says there is more to sex than that.

When you make love to your wife (or if you are single, as you anticipate that day), do you sense the "spiritual mystery" in those moments as two Christ followers in a committed, covered marriage? The spiritual elements of marital sex have to be considered in light of Scripture. So is there any "spiritual mystery" in masturbation or is it more just "physical fact"?

Does masturbation "avoid commitment"?

Does masturbation "avoid intimacy"?

When masturbation is completed, does the act leave the person feeling "more lonely than ever"?

Is masturbation the kind of sex that can "never become one?"

If God created your sexual being solely to create enjoyment with your wife, is masturbation "a violation of the sacredness of your own body?"

Is masturbation an example of "God-given and God-modeled love?"

Let's go back to our earlier discussion of Jesus' definition of lust and purity in Matthew 5. I believe we could all agree that masturbation involves the imagining of a sex act with someone. If you are single, that is sex outside of marriage. If you are married, that is adultery. Every scenario applied to the mental aspect of masturbation violates Jesus' adultery teaching *and* Paul's teaching on sex.

Here are three lies the Enemy tells men about masturbation:

1. It's just a natural way to relieve your sexual tension.

2. It will help you control your sex drive.

3. It won't affect your marriage or your future marriage.

Even young men quickly begin to see these simply are not true. In fact, they most often create the opposite effect.

From a spiritual and scriptural standpoint, a major issue with masturbation is that the act:

- Allows you to meet needs intended for only your wife or future wife to meet

- Isolates your sexual world that God intended to be shared in marriage

- Violates God's intention for your body and sexuality

To cover the base, I have had men ask if masturbation is okay if sex with your wife is what you imagine. Well, read 1 Corinthians 6 again and answer that. Plus, if you are married, isn't that a strangely ironic way to have sex "with her"?

I want to be very clear that my only goal on this topic is to offer you a biblical perspective on what is *never* taught or talked about in Christian settings. As with all the topics we will address in these pages, I want to give you evidence you may have never heard before. Then just ask you to do exactly what God does with us all: make your own decision on how to respond. God is always a gentleman and never forces His ways on us. So we should not attempt to do that to each other either.

I made a decision many years ago that I never debate anyone on anything. I will discuss and answer questions all day long, but debate, no. My primary motive comes from the fact that I have never met anyone who became a Christian or surrendered any area of his/her life to the Lord because he/she was debated into obedience. No one ever gave his testimony to say, "I became a Christian when I lost an argument," or

"Yeah, this guy out-shouted me so I had no choice but to ask Jesus into my life."

I am not including the art of apologetics in this explanation. There is a place for offering a compelling case of facts for someone to be able to make an informed decision, but that is a very different animal than arguing and debating faith issues.

I had an older man walk up to me after an event and tell me that his wife had died and because he is still a healthy, normal man, he had a pass from God on masturbation. He said he did not hear anything in my teaching that took away his "exemption." I smiled and responded, "I respect your right to make your own call on that issue." And I do. And that is that. If he was ready for an argument, I disappointed him. (But if he was truly convinced he was in the clear with God, then why feel the need to tell me He was?)

If you are a dad with a son, I want to encourage you to have this difficult conversation with him at the age you feel appropriate. Yes, bringing up this subject is one of the most awkward things you will ever talk about. I get it. I did with my two sons. But if you can establish that there are no topics off limits *now* and show your son you will have the guts to deal with the tough subjects with him and answer *any* question, you will establish a close, transparent relationship for now and down the road. He will feel like he can come to you about anything and you will handle the issue respectfully and honestly with him.

Over time, that level of open and honest communication can make your boys into godly men by encouraging them not to hide but be open. You want them to understand that no subject is unapproachable with you and nothing is impossible for God. In fact, I want to encourage you to eventually bring up *every* topic in this book with your sons.

Trading Lust for Lordship

To close this tough subject matter, when you study *all* the Scriptures regarding sexual purity, everything about masturbation seems to violate the spirit of those passages. The foundational truth being that God meant for our sexual lives to be experienced only inside the sanctity of marriage—not with anyone else before or during and certainly not alone to exclude our spouse.

Check out this passage, especially the last verse:

That is why I say to run from sex sin. No other sin affects the body as this one does. When you sin this sin it is against your own body. Haven't you yet learned that your body is the home of the Holy Spirit God gave you, and that he lives within you? Your own body does not belong to you. For God has bought you with a great price. So use every part of your body to give glory back to God because he owns it. (1 Corinthians 6:18–20 TLB)

What if we agreed to Paul's charge? What if you decided to once and for all give *"every part of your body"* to God because of all He has done for you? What if you prayed, "Lord, this flesh is all Yours. I want to only please You, not myself." What would change about your life? What might start? What might stop?

The irony about these questions is that when we give our lives to Christ, we are supposed to be agreeing with these decisions already. Somehow we have managed to make all biblical mandates into options. But the amazing thing about Jesus is He always allows for fresh starts and new beginnings any day, anytime, no matter what we have done in the past or what state our mind or life is in.

What might happen if all the men who say they follow Jesus gave up their steady diet of lust and porn and began to spend the *same amount of time* in God's Word?

Do you think that would change anything? Would thoughts become different? Would actions be different? Would life get better or worse if we decided to live God's way? (Brother Paul, you have anything to say about this?)

And that means killing off everything connected with that way of death: sexual promiscuity, impurity, lust, doing whatever you feel like whenever you feel like it, and grabbing whatever attracts your fancy. That's a life shaped by things and feelings instead of by God. It's because of this kind of thing that God is about to explode in anger. It wasn't long ago that you were doing all that stuff and not knowing any better. But you know better now, so make sure it's all gone for good: bad temper, irritability, meanness, profanity, dirty talk. (Colossians 3:5–8 MSG)

Listen, brother, you can win this battle!

Maybe you have told yourself you can't.

Maybe the Enemy keeps telling you that you can't.

But you can address your hurts and needs, face yourself, take your thoughts captive, and end the sin that is hurting your soul, while taking up actions that glorify God and satisfy your spirit like you never thought possible.

*So if you're serious about living
this new resurrection life with Christ, act like it.
Pursue the things over which Christ presides.
Don't shuffle along, eyes to the ground,
absorbed with the things right in front of you.
Look up, and be alert to what is going on
around Christ—that's where the action is.
See things from his perspective.
Your old life is dead. Your new life,
which is your real life
—even though invisible to spectators
—is with Christ in God.
He is your life.
When Christ (your real life, remember)
shows up again on this earth,
you'll show up, too—the real you, the glorious you.
Meanwhile, be content with obscurity, like Christ.*
(Colossians 3:1–4 MSG)

Chapter Seven

Seven Steps Toward Purity

Christian brothers, keep your minds thinking
about whatever is true,
whatever is respected, whatever is right,
whatever is pure,
whatever can be loved,
and whatever is well thought of.
If there is anything good and worth giving thanks for,
think about these things.
—Philippians 4:8 NLV

Here are seven practical steps that can help you in your personal purity. While we will certainly never arrive at perfection this side of Heaven, we can move closer and closer to the image of our Lord and Example, Jesus Christ.

1—Admit to and Deal with Sin

As in most step programs for addiction, members are told they must first acknowledge there is a problem. That is true of all sin. So much of our disobedience is rooted in denial, rationale, and excuses. We must have a desire to change the behavior, and agree with God that we have wronged Him and that the sin is harmful for us. That sense of conviction and confession should drive us toward God, not away from Him.

For the kind of sorrow God wants us to experience leads us away from sin and results in salvation. There's no regret for that kind of sorrow. (2 Corinthians 7:10)

The Lord isn't really being slow about his promise, as some people think. No, he is being patient for your sake. He does not want anyone to be destroyed, but wants everyone to repent. (2 Peter 3:9)

This first step is straightforward. Face up. Own up. Realize. Admit. Then . . .

2—Confess Your Sin/Disobedience

But if we confess our sins, he will forgive our sins, because we can trust God to do what is right. He will cleanse us from all the wrongs we have done. (1 John 1:9 NCV)

Look at what we are asked to do: Confess. Get honest. Be open. Come clean. Agree with God that our actions are wrong.

Then look at what Christ will do: Forgive completely as if the sin had never happened. He will do the right thing by us, providing what we need. He will fully and completely cleanse us from *all* wrongs. Once we confess, we can let go of the guilt, shame, and regret to trust that we are now clean through and through. Leave the sin and any connected guilt with God and walk back into our life, accepting that we are forgiven.

3—Un-isolate Yourself

Our culture has fully embraced isolation, particularly in regard to avoiding actual face-to-face interaction. Far too many men today are not connected to anyone. Sometimes that includes their own families. If they got into trouble at 3:00 p.m. or 3:00 a.m., they would struggle to figure out someone to call for help.

As men, we isolate because of our pride. So to un-isolate and connect will mean we have to allow God to humble us. Let our guard down. To have real friends, not virtual online friends, we must first be real friends. We must become the man whom we would want as a friend. We have to be vulnerable and open our hearts for change to come.

Ninety-nine percent of the men who have ever come to me for help in trying to escape any sin or addiction were isolated. But even coming to me was the first step toward interaction and out of isolation. Then we could go to God together and get a plan.

Turn to me and have mercy, for I am alone and in deep distress. My problems go from bad to worse. Oh, save me from them all! Feel my pain and see my trouble. Forgive all my sins. (Psalm 25:16–18)

The more open a man becomes, the healthier he can get, and the more un-isolated he is.

4—Accountability

Why do step program members of any kind not only confess in front of the group, but also commit to regularly attend the meetings? Because accountability has been created, and for it to keep working, consistency is key. The meetings along with the connections are the catalyst for continued change and victory. "If I mess up during the week, I *have* to tell the group. If I have a great week, I *get* to tell the group."

Where would our Armed Forces be without accountability? Police? Doctors? The judicial system? What keeps everyone from taking whatever they want from whomever they want, whenever they want? Accountability. This social dynamic is built into our lives all around us, so it makes sense to build it on a spiritual level for the sake of our survival and success over the long haul.

Aside from being married to a godly woman, having a small group of guys who decide to get serious and be accountable to one another is the most powerful agent of change I have seen for men to grow in their faith in Christ and defeat the work of the Enemy in their lives. Being honest about sin and temptation with brothers who will relate, understand, pray for you, and believe in you to change is a powerful force of Christ-like love.

We also need brothers to talk us out of sin when we are tempted, and then if we go through with it can help us stop the condemnation attack, talk it out, confess, and pray. This is a major key to lasting success over sin. To be clear, I am not talking about making anyone your priest, but rather each of you becoming pastors to one another.

Iron is made sharp with iron, and one man is made sharp by a friend. (Proverbs 27:17 NLV)

We have all seen how ineffective the flippant, "Hey, buddy, thanks for sharing. I'll pray for you," has been in our church culture after we have slammed down a stack of pancakes together in the fellowship hall and run out the door. But a group of three men who meet regularly and give one another permission to get into each other's lives for the sake of maturity as a Christ follower has a high rate of success for real life change.

I once heard a man give his testimony at an event. He explained the way his wife figured out he was having an affair was by looking at his calendar. She asked him to explain where he was at certain times while away from the house and on certain trips. Bottom line was there was far too much time away from home that was *unaccounted for.*

We will cover accountability again in the final chapter as a function of a men's small group, but I wanted to introduce the subject in the context of developing purity in your life. There is also a list of men's small group accountability questions in the back of this book.

5—Develop Principles for Offense and Defense

"But principled people hold tight, keep a firm grip on life, sure that their clean, pure hands will get stronger and stronger!" (Job 17:9 MSG)

A thick bankroll is no help when life falls apart, but a principled life can stand up to the worst. (Proverbs 11:4 MSG)

The thinking of principled people makes for justice; the plots of degenerates corrupt. (Proverbs 12:5 MSG)

A principle is a simple rule you set for yourself for the purpose of protection (defense) or growth (offense). This can help you make a decision once and stick to it, rather than trying to decide in the midst of a temptation or a crisis. Some principles are just for a season, while some are for a lifetime.

Now that you have confessed your sin and see your areas of shortcoming, look at any situation, place, or person that causes you to be tempted. Put principles in place to protect yourself from that circumstance. Then give your principles to your accountability partners. You can also give a list to your wife. If you have an older son, it would be cool to share it with him too.

Listen carefully to my wisdom; take to heart what I can teach you. You'll treasure its sweetness deep within; you'll give it bold expression in your speech. To make sure your foundation is trust in GOD, I'm laying it all out right now just for you. I'm giving you thirty sterling principles—tested guidelines to live by. Believe me—these are truths that work, and will keep you accountable to those who sent you. (Proverbs 22:17 MSG)

Like accountability, we will cover principles again in the final chapter as a function of a men's small group, but I wanted to introduce the subject here in the context of developing purity in your life.

6—Detox Your Mind

If you do a detox or detoxification diet, you stop eating all the bad stuff and eat only small portions of good stuff for a set time. A typical detox diet involves drinking only water and eating only select amounts of fruit, vegetables, and nuts. The bottom line is you radically change what you have been putting into your body to cleanse your system. Typically, weight loss will be a by-product of the effort.

A mental and spiritual detox involves radically changing what you put into your *mind*. Write down anything that is placing negative, tempting, or un-Christlike images into your thoughts, such as the internet, social media, news, computer, phone, TV, movies, games, magazines, books, and certain people and situations. Set a specific span of time for you to stop or seriously limit your time with those elements. For example, between work and outside of work, you figure you waste a couple of hours a day on the computer. Cut out all that time for a while. Do you tend to watch TV shows that create temptation? Stop them for a time. Are you and a buddy (or your wife) not very discriminating about the movies you see? Stop for a season.

The goal here is not to become a religious zealot, but to disrupt your normal patterns so you can give your mind and heart a break from your usual diet of input. Figure out where the Enemy is getting in the door. Replace as much of this time as possible with time in God's Word and prayer. You may find within a week to two, you have started some new, healthier habits. You may find that there are some things you can easily live without and that this exercise has improved the quality of your spiritual and emotional health.

For we are the temple of the living God. As God said: "I will live in them and walk among them. I will be their God, and they

will be my people. Therefore, come out from among unbeliev-
ers, and separate yourselves from them, says the LORD. Don't
touch their filthy things, and I will welcome you. And I will be
your Father, and you will be my sons and daughters, says the
LORD Almighty." Because we have these promises, dear friends,
let us cleanse ourselves from everything that can defile our body
or spirit. And let us work toward complete holiness because we
fear God. (2 Corinthians 6:16–7:1)

The spirit of this passage from Paul is obedience and action
for the sake of holiness. That is what the detox concept is
all about.

7—The Principle of Replacement

Regardless of how godly we become, we are still only human.
If we look at our lives through the filter of all these things
we must stop or not do, we will eventually either exasper-
ate ourselves or become legalistic or both. I believe that for
everything God asks us to give up for Him, He will replace it
with something so much better.

"Which of you, if his son asks for bread, will give him a stone?
Or if he asks for a fish, will give him a snake? If you, then, though
you are evil, know how to give good gifts to your children, how
much more will your Father in heaven give good gifts to those
who ask him!" (Matthew 7:9–11 NIV)

If a guy spends two hours every night at a bar and decides to
quit drinking, he better figure out what he is going to do with
the newfound two hours placed back into his schedule or he'll
just end up back at the bar again. We must pray and ask God

to help us replace the things we give up with good things from Him. He will help us replace our stuff with His stuff, but we have to ask Him, listen, and look for His answers. Healthy hobbies can keep us from terrible temptations.

Here is another example: You are a single guy and the girl you have been dating is not helping you live pure. You have talked to her about your sexual convictions, but that seems to just fuel the fire. You know you have to break up with her. You get accountability to break up, stay away, and stop communication. You hung out with her a minimum of fifteen hours a week. Decide immediately what you will fill that time with.

Do you need to start working out again? Is there a hobby or sport you have wanted to learn? A buddy or two you have been neglecting because of her? Is there a volunteering opportunity you have always said you would like to help with? Bottom line is if you find yourself sitting alone with an extra fifteen hours on your hands, there is a strong likelihood you will phone her up or get into trouble of some other kind. So you must plan on doing good. Pray and ask the Lord for guidance on what to do.

I chose to give an example for a single guy on this one, but married guys, you get it. You can apply this same concept to anything you give up. A married man may have less time to get in trouble, but many have proven over and over again that will not necessarily stop us.

This concept that God not only will but also wants to give us new things from Him is seen throughout Scripture. Here is a beautiful statement of love and promise that God made to

Israel and makes available to you and me today. Look at the number of offers made to us just in three simple verses.

I will sprinkle clean water on you, and you will be clean; I will cleanse you from all your impurities and from all your idols. I will give you a new heart and put a new spirit in you; I will remove from you your heart of stone and give you a heart of flesh. And I will put my Spirit in you and move you to follow my decrees and be careful to keep my laws. (Ezekiel 36:25–27 NIV)

Additional Principles to Purity

• No second looks.

The first look is just the recognition of a person. But in that split-second, if your brain tells you it is an attractive woman and you make the choice to look again, the second look is the problem. If the second look becomes a stare, well, then it can quickly escalate into what Jesus warned us of. The incredible aspect is this can happen in milliseconds. Many men train themselves for the second look; they are going to do it every time. But the great news is the training can go the other way when our minds become transformed to never take the second look.

Read what Job said in 31:1 when he was suffering and working to prove his innocence before God: *"I made a covenant with my eyes not to look lustfully at a young woman" (NIV).*

• Treat every older woman as if she were your mother and every younger girl/woman as if she were your sister/daughter.

I had a man come up to me after I had taught this principle in a purity session, and he said he had recently been at a store and got into a conversation with a young woman. He realized he was beginning to flirt with her. He said in the very next moment, he heard the Lord say to him, "She's the same age as your granddaughter." He said, "So I stopped and told her, 'Great talking with you,' and I walked away. I will never forget that moment."

As we discussed earlier, isn't it interesting how if a guy actually does try to flirt with one of the significant women in our family, we just want to destroy the jerk. So we have to apply the same rule to ourselves, because every female is someone's daughter, mother, niece, or granddaughter.

- Commit to turn your eyes and heart fully to your bride.

Where the heart is, the eyes will follow. Where the eyes go, the heart will follow. If our eyes are looking elsewhere, it is not an issue with our wives, but an issue with our hearts.

- Always act as if your wife were either with you or watching you.

How many interactions, brief or lengthy, would we *not* have if our wives were with us? This principle is great to keep us in check anywhere, anytime, with anyone.

Modus Operandi

All of our decisions are born in our hearts. But the embryo from which all decisions grow is called a motive. Motives are tricky elements in our lives. We can do something that looks very nice, very good, and harmless, but we can do it completely with the wrong motive.

The kind of purity the New Testament teaches us is driven by our motives flowing fully out of total submission to Christ. What is it that drove Christ in the garden, and throughout the trials, the beatings, the whipping with the cat-of-nine-tails, the walk up to Golgotha with the cross, the nails through the wrists, the nails through the feet, and the hours in agony trying not to suffocate hanging on the cross? What drove Him to give up His life to the Father as a final sacrifice for all sin? The answer: His *motive* of love for you and me!

All we can be capable of in our sin, death, and flesh is more sin, death, and flesh. We are not able to produce life, love, joy, peace, patience, kindness, goodness, gentleness, or self-control. We cannot have pure motives, attitudes, or actions on our own power and strength. That is what drove Christ to the cross. To change all that so we could become what we believe.

For these reasons, God is ultimately after our motives—to make them His, to make them pure, to radically change us from the inside out, and to make all things new.

Let's pray:

"Merciful and gracious God, we thank You that You have provided a path to purity, in our actions, attitudes, and even our motives. Give us the sense to surrender when we are defeated, the wisdom to turn to You and obey, the grace to forgive ourselves as You forgive us, and the boldness to move forward in Your freedom. May each day bring greater victory over the places in us where we have allowed the Enemy to set up camp. May we defeat and remove him from our lives. Then please take possession of every part of our hearts, so we can know You in the fullness and intimacy that You dreamed of when You hung on the cross and redeemed our sin. Give us the daily desire to seek Your purity in our lives as we move forward into pursuing truth in our hearts. In the name of Jesus, amen."

Part Two

Believing,
Becoming,
Being
a Man of Truth

Chapter Eight

Truth Seeker, Lie Detector

The mouth of the righteous man utters wisdom,
and his tongue speaks what is just.
—Psalm 37:30 NIV

If you get any group of guys in a room that are even somewhat comfortable with one another to start talking about "stupid things I have said," the responses will range from total shock to hysterical laughter. You'll hear comments like, "Man, I cannot believe you said that! What were you thinking?" and "Did you not have any idea how that was going to sound?"

I have a good friend whose wife often tells him, "Honey, your mouth lives by 'Ready. Fire. Aim.'" A clever description of the fact that while our tongue may have a safety on its trigger, many of us rarely activate it. Therefore, we can get in trouble by:

- What we say that we shouldn't

- What we don't say that we should

Some of the greatest regrets we will deal with over the course of our lives are:

- Words we never should have said

- Words we should have spoken but never did

- Words that were spoken too soon

- Words that were spoken too late

- Words that had truth but no grace

- Words that had grace but no truth

A very small but major part of the body needs to be redeemed *daily*—the tongue. We have to come to grips with realizing that as men our mouths need a lot of help. Our speech desperately needs balance.

The phrase "bite your tongue" speaks to the very practical action that if you place the end of it between your upper and lower teeth, you literally cannot speak. Make sounds, yes; be understood, no. Plus if you bite down a bit harder, you then focus more on the pain created, which can make you forget about what you wanted to say that you shouldn't! A practice of some kings was if a messenger brought bad news or information he was concerned might not remain a secret, he would have the man's tongue cut out.

The Bible says a lot about our speech, but focuses an entire passage on the tongue.

In the same way, the tongue is a small thing that makes grand speeches. But a tiny spark can set a great forest on fire. And among all the parts of the body, the tongue is a flame of fire. It is a whole world of wickedness, corrupting your entire body. It can set your whole life on fire, for it is set on fire by hell itself. People can tame all kinds of animals, birds, reptiles, and fish, but no one can tame the tongue. It is restless and evil, full of deadly poison. (James 3:5–8)

How many times have we wished for a filter that would stop our thoughts between our brain and our tongue? Many times in life we can only hope for some sort of censoring to deem whether a thought is fit to proceed out of our mouths. As for me, I have another major issue attached to this speech problem. I don't just have trouble with *what* I say, but *how* I say it. That is exactly why after we begin our journey toward purity, the very next issue to battle is our tongue.

You have to love how bluntly honest David always was with God. The shepherd-king's transparency should be an encouragement to us in our own prayers.

I said to myself, "I will watch what I do and not sin in what I say. I will hold my tongue when the ungodly are around me." But as I stood there in silence—not even speaking of good things—the turmoil within me grew worse. The more I thought about it, the hotter I got, igniting a fire of words. (Psalm 39:1–3)

Overflow of the Heart

Here are some scenarios that can reveal through our words what is actually in our hearts:

- Hitting your thumb *hard* with a hammer

- Getting cut off in traffic when you are running late

- Finding out a coworker or church member gossiped about you

- Having someone in your family pop off with a cutting remark

The sudden in-the-moment actions are far better gauges of our purity than when we are given time for a calculated response.

My wife and I often drive from Nashville to Chattanooga to see her family. Interstate 24 East goes up, across, and down Monteagle, a mountain and town of the same name that sits at the top. As you climb the steep grade along the way, in numerous places as you cut through the high canyon walls, there are large streams of water literally gushing straight out of the rocks and crashing down beside the road. The water often looks more like it is being shot from a fire hose than flowing from a waterfall.

Every time, those majestic scenes are powerful and beautiful. We never see the source of the water, only what is flowing out and the sheer force of energy being created hour after hour, day after day. Every time I see that mountain spring water gushing from cracks in the rock face, I think of Jesus' words in Luke 6:45: *"Whatever is in the heart overflows into speech"* (TLB).

Our lives are like those rocks. People cannot see into our hearts—the source—yet when they hear us speak, they experience our words like water pouring out, our overflow, and get a glimpse of who we are. The proof is we change our perceptions of people all the time after hearing them speak—for better and for worse. We can meet someone and within minutes either be drawn to them or repelled by them simply by their words.

Now here's some good news: As Christ followers, we have the opportunity every day to surrender our hearts, mouths, and tongues to Christ. Like any other aspect of our spiritual lives, the more we learn to submit, the better we can be at communication.

We have to constantly take an honest look at what is over-flowing from our hearts. Not what we *think* we are communicating or *assume* we sound like to people. What vibe do we regularly give off in communication—the verbal and the nonverbal? We have to ask ourselves: Do I speak differently at home than the workplace? Do I speak to my kids different-ly than I do the people at church? Do I honor my wife when I speak to her and speak to others about her? (These are also great accountability questions to ask each other in our men's small groups, customized to your particular struggles.)

Discomfort Zones

- Learning the balance of speech is the gaining of wisdom, available only through Christ who can teach us:
  o When to use our words
  o When not to use our words
  o How to say the right thing in the right way
  o How to avoid saying the wrong thing

I have found the older I get, the quieter I become. I have always been an introvert who has learned to be extroverted for the sake of ministry and my career. But that effort takes a lot of energy out of me. Yet I believe growing quieter is not a change in my personality as much as gaining wisdom and experience. It is one thing to speak less but quite another to listen more. Proactively listening with intention to truly hear what someone is saying. I remember as a much-younger man watching older men I respected and thinking, *He has so much wisdom. Why doesn't he say more?* I have a much better understanding of that dynamic now.

As our culture grows more self-focused and dependent on screens over being face-to-face, people are losing their ability to actually listen and hear what others are saying. I can tell when someone is just waiting for me to stop talking so they can say what they are busy thinking. So why not just shut up and let them get started if I am wasting my breath anyway?

- The balance of speech is to know the right words to say with the right timing.

One of the biggest defenses I hear from guys regarding their communication is, "Well, but that's my personality. That's just how I am. Everybody knows that."

Honestly, making that declaration is most often just an excuse for bad behavior. Such a response shouts out that he needs everyone to understand that he is not going to change, so everyone in his life better just line up with him.

God gave each of us a very distinct and unique personality. Like snowflakes and fingerprints, we each have our unique and detailed make-up, so our Father wants us to be who He made us to be. However, as disciples of Jesus, we should allow Him to overtake our personality, whether extroverted or introverted, loud or quiet, high energy or laid-back. Slide over to the passenger seat and let Him be the driving force behind our character and speech.

- Christ alone, not our personalities, should be the gatekeeper of our mouths.

Jesus can help extroverts learn when to shut up and listen. He can teach introverts when to speak up and say what is on their minds. He, not our flesh, becomes the Source of the overflow. Our personality can simply become the unique way we express Jesus in us through our words, actions, and attitudes.

I have seen God clearly call men to certain roles that will stretch their personal boundaries. I have witnessed some guys inventory their personality and decide they cannot grow out of their current state. Their answer often lies in whether or not to take the risk of climbing out of their comfort zones.

To be effective ministers of the gospel, to which *every* disciple is called, we have to surrender personality to the Lordship of Christ and allow Him to empower us to do His will and work in His way, not ours. Regardless of our personality type or our comfort levels with people, that process is going to be uncomfortable on some level. God wants to continually use and stretch us in who we are. He wants to see us grow throughout our lives. That simply requires us to be *available*; it is not so much about us being *able*.

I have an important question for you: Have you ever told God no to something because you felt the assignment did not fit your personality? Have you ever reminded Him of your personality type and why the request He is giving you just will not work because of how *He* made you? (Think about that one.)

One of the areas where we must be really careful is at church. Countless times I have seen people offered positions only *because* of their personality, not their gifting or spiritual maturity. Someone with the gift of teaching may be placed on parking-lot duty because he appears to be an extreme introvert, when in reality he is a deep thinker. Someone with an outgoing personality is offered a leadership position when in reality they have little knowledge of Scripture. Just because we feel a certain role should have a certain personality does not mean God has willed that decision. That caution is as much about individual members knowing their gifts as it is about church leaders choosing people to fill roles.

Here are some common scenarios: "He's just so good with people. He needs to be teaching Sunday school." Someone who is "good with people" is not necessarily a good teacher of Scripture. Or "He wants to be in the Easter musical, but we'll let him help backstage. He's too quiet to be given a character role." All this does is keep people in their boxes, while God is about challenging us all out of our boxes and into relying on Him!

Truth from the Inside Out

In John 14:6, Jesus referred to Himself as the Truth, therefore we can discern from His statement that:

- As Truth, Jesus is the only Source from which *all* truth flows.

We will find truth by no other means, except through Christ. Searching inside our own hearts, the ways of the world, or through the many belief systems of the ages will not produce truth. Many other belief systems' truths that are correct are just borrowed from Scripture. Because that is where Truth began and is still the only Source.

- As Truth, Jesus is the Destroyer of lies.

In John 8:44, Jesus called Satan "the father of lies." We must pay attention to the fact that this is the only time the Enemy is referred to as a father. Where Jesus is, the truth resides, therefore where no lies exist. As His truth penetrates us, He can then destroy the Enemy's lies. But Christ will not take them from you. You have to hand them over.

Think of the transfer like this: You are dangling off the side of a cliff holding onto a rope for dear life. Yet the harder you try to pull yourself up, the more you keep falling farther down. You continue to hang on and hope for help. Finally, another rope suddenly appears beside you. You look up to see Jesus holding the other end. You grab His rope with your other hand.

As He begins to pull you up, you are still holding the other rope with your other hand. Now you are being pulled between the two directions. What do you have to do? Let go of the old rope and grab His with both hands, of course. Not only will Christ's truth lift you up, but it will also set you free from the lies holding you down that are keeping you in a dangerous place.

As we grow in a personal relationship with Christ, we are spending time with Truth. As we pray, listen, and read His Word, we are interacting with Truth. The more we engage, the more we take in Truth and let go of lies. We all know that players tend to perform at the level of their coaching. The more you spend time with Christ, the more you allow Him access into your motives, thoughts, attitudes, words, and actions. The more Truth you allow in, the more Truth becomes a part of who you are.

The bottom line: Spend time with liars—learn to lie. Spend time with Truth—learn the truth.

> *The believer replied, "Every promise of God proves true;*
> *he protects everyone who runs to him for help.*
> *So don't second-guess him; he might take you to task*
> *and show up your lies." And then he prayed,*
> *"God, I'm asking for two things before I die;*
> *don't refuse me—Banish lies from my lips*
> *and liars from my presence."*
> *(Proverbs 30:5–7 MSG)*

Chapter Nine

Habits, Half-Truths, and Hostages

As Samuel grew up, the LORD was with him,
and everything Samuel said proved to be reliable.
—1 Samuel 3:19

So how do we believe we can become and be men of truth?

- **To be men of truth, we must get rid of the lies we tell ourselves.**

We all have lies we have come to believe. It is just a matter of how many and how severe they are. But those lies are road-blocks to achieving real growth and freedom in life.

Lies may have been said to you by someone in your past like a family member, coach, teacher, or schoolmate. You may have come to believe a lie that you invented with no one's help. A lie may have been said only once to you and had a deep impact, or maybe one was repeated to you again and again for years. Someone else may have been the original source of a lie, but now you have become the perpetrator because you keep repeating the lie every day. You no longer hear the original person's voice, only yours.

The first and crucial step is to recognize the lies. This can be tough to discern because some lies can become such a part of us that we have convinced ourselves they are actually true. Like the old high school or college buddy who always got you into trouble, but you could just never seem to tell him to take a hike. That is what these lies may have become for you—comfortable, but catastrophic.

Here are some common lies we tell ourselves:

I'm no good.	I won't ever amount to anything.
I'm stupid.	I'm ugly.
I'm not as good as everyone else.	I can't be forgiven.
What I feel doesn't matter.	I can't be loved.
I don't count.	God won't bless me.

Going deep and being brutally honest, circle any of the ones above you believe and then take a moment to think through and write down any other lies you tell yourself:

_____

_____

_____

_____

_____

_____

A major source of the condemnation, judgment, accusations, and lies we have in our hearts and minds come from the Enemy. His rock gushes so much that it can drown us!

"For the Accuser of our brothers has been thrown down from heaven onto earth—he accused them day and night before our God." (Revelation 12:10 TLB)

I once heard James Robison, the legendary pastor, president of Life Outreach International, and TV host, share in a message that after decades of preaching and teaching to millions of people, still today while speaking, from inside his own mind he still regularly hears accusations such as, "You talk too long," "They aren't listening to you," "You're putting people to sleep," and "You aren't as good of a speaker as their pastor." Everyone assumes a man like Robison would feel nothing but incredible confidence when he stands to speak. Yet the decades of ministry and millions of people have not silenced that voice of accusation trying to distract him from ministry.

Notice that Revelation 12:10 calls Satan "the accuser of our brothers." We need to ask: Who are the brothers? Well, right now, that is us. And what does Satan do? He accuses, blames, and levels his charges against us 24/7. Day and night means he *never* stops.

"It has come at last—salvation and power and the Kingdom of our God, and the authority of his Christ. . . . And they have defeated him by the blood of the Lamb and by their testimony." (Revelation 12:10–11)

So to defeat the lies of the Enemy, Christ has given us:

- Salvation

- Power

- The kingdom of God

- The authority of Christ

- The blood of the Lamb

- Our personal testimony of what God has done in us and for us

These are the spiritual weapons we can wield to let go of lies and grab hold of truth.

The word of our testimony is what we speak about Christ. If I give a testimony, I am telling what Christ has done for me. The truth about Jesus in us overcomes the Enemy's accusations of us. For us all, there is a lot of bad we can say about ourselves and it would be true. But we are no longer basing our lives on us as well as our reputations, but on Christ and His! His authority and shed blood changes us and also defeats Satan.

Regardless of the source of our lies—whether Satan, someone else, our own voice, or all three—we would love for the truth of Christ to invade our lies, take over, and then just supernaturally we stop believing them. But that is not how it works. Christ wants us to lay them down before Him and choose to take up His truth in their place. Jesus will never break down a door; He will only walk through the ones we open.

Here is a practical exercise that can help us replace lies by using God's Word:

Old Lie: "You'll never amount to anything."

New Truth: *"Now you are no longer a slave but God's own child. And since you are his child, God has made you his heir"* (Galatians 4:7).

Personalize: "I am no longer a slave, but a son; and since I am a son, God has made me His heir."

Old Lie: "My sin is unforgiveable."

New Truth: *"He is so rich in kindness and grace that he purchased our freedom with the blood of his Son and forgave our sins. He has showered his kindness on us, along with all wisdom and understanding"* (Ephesians 1:7–8).

Personalize: "In Christ I have redemption through His blood and the forgiveness of sins, with the riches of God's grace He gives me all His wisdom and understanding."

Using your list from a few pages back, write down each lie with which you struggle to let go. Find a truth in Scripture that refutes and replaces your lie. You can use Bible Gateway to search keywords in your favorite version. Follow the pattern above and then keep what you write down in a place where you will see it regularly. Read, memorize, and meditate on your verses. You worked very hard over many years to teach yourself the lies. Now work just as hard to take in the new truth God offers you.

The three R's to ridding yourself of lies and embracing truth are:

1. Refute: Deny their power over you and confess they are false.

2. Repent: Turn away from the lies and toward God in a one-eighty about-face.

3. Replace: Using the above exercise, put a new truth from God in the place of the old lie. Personalize it for you.

Following Jesus' baptism, He went into the desert alone to fast and pray for forty days to prepare for His ministry. Satan showed up three times to try to take advantage of the opportunity. Jesus' only defense was to use Scripture, specifically verses from Deuteronomy, to combat the Enemy. Therefore, the best way for us to stop the Enemy's lies is also with God's Word. Look at the first encounter in Matthew 4:3–4:

During that time the devil came and said to him, "If you are the Son of God, tell these stones to become loaves of bread." But Jesus told him, "No! The Scriptures say, 'People do not live by bread alone, but by every word that comes from the mouth of God.'"

- **To be men of truth, we must get rid of the lies we tell others.**

  o Lies: These are false statements, untruths, and deceptions. We all understand this one.

  o Embellishments: We embellish when we try to make the story sound better than what actually happened.

We add to or expand on the truth using lies. This is the classic fish story: You caught a one-foot catfish, which eventually became a two-foot bass. Another classic example is when we make ourselves sound a lot tougher or confrontational than we actually were: "So then I told him, 'Listen, bud, you better back off now,'" when in reality, what was said was, "Uh, excuse me, sir, but I really don't appreciate that."

Embellishments are usually our expressing what we wish we would have done or said or what the outcome would have been. Once a story gets past the facts, we have to accept that we are lying.

o Half-truths: A half-truth is only telling part of the story to cover our own butt. We leave out any incriminating facts. An example would be showing up late to a meeting and saying, "So sorry, I ran into a bad traffic jam." The truth is there was a bad traffic jam, but you also left fifteen minutes late. Remember, if you tell a half-truth, then the half you left out means you lied by omission.

o Patronizations: We patronize when we tell people what we believe they want to hear just to appease or manipulate the situation. We normally use patronizations to get our way or deflect the blame from us. An example would be, "I really want you to partner with me on this project because you are just so creative with awesome ideas." The truth: "I'm so far behind on my deadline that I don't have a clue how I can finish without help, and you're probably the only one who will."

When a man struggles regularly with one or more of these issues, he tends to get worse over time. If he learns that half-truths will get him by and keep him out of trouble with his wife, he tends to retain the pattern. If he embellishes stories with the same crowd, then the stories have to get bigger and better to get the same reaction. If he learns to patronize his family or his coworkers, the manipulation has to get stronger over time to keep the same effect. Each of these can become actual addictions in a man's speech. He gets to the point where he cannot stop creating them.

The LORD detests lying lips, but he delights in those who tell the truth. (Proverbs 12:22)

- **To be men of truth, we must rid ourselves of unforgiveness.**

Over generations, this single area has derailed millions of men for many years of their lives because they have refused to forgive just one person. And all too often, the one eventually becomes a growing list of people. Not forgiving others can gather more unforgiveness as quickly as a duct tape ball can gather lint.

Choosing to not forgive people is like taking them hostage. As the bitterness sets in, we abduct the person and tie them to the chair of their offense. The hideout where we keep our hostages is our own heart, covertly tucked away. Most people will never know that we are keeping people locked up in there.

Here is the horrible plot twist though: The person or people we won't forgive is not actually who is tied up in the chair after all. They are not actually the hostages. We are the hostages. We are the ones bound up. We are the one in hiding. Our offender is out walking the streets in total freedom—rarely, if ever, thinking about us. But he/she is on our mind daily.

But the only cure for unforgiveness is forgiveness.

Our culture has wanted us to believe for far too long that unforgiveness and being calloused is a man's right to be right. How many times have you seen a family divided over a man not letting go of his pride? But a Christ follower has no choice but to forgive.

"If you forgive those who sin against you, your heavenly Father will forgive you. But if you refuse to forgive others, your Father will not forgive your sins." (Matthew 6:14–15)

As always regarding all truth in life, the Lord was quite clear on where He stands on this issue, so to follow Him, we have to fall in line. But the amazing thing is He knows that living in a state of forgiveness is the best thing for us. We must not only say we believe in forgiveness; we must *be* forgiven and *become* an example of His forgiveness to everyone around us.

Jesus said to the people who believed in him, "You are truly my disciples if you remain faithful to my teachings. And you will know the truth, and the truth will set you free." (John 8:31–32)

Chapter Ten

Getting Angry God's Way

My Christian brothers, you know everyone should listen much and speak little. He should be slow to become angry.
—James 1:19 NLV

Anger is a natural emotion we can experience without sinning. There are many instances in Scripture where God got angry with His people. The religious leaders often angered Jesus. Then there is the well-known scene in the temple with the moneychangers where He cleaned house. Yet neither God nor Jesus ever sinned. Here is the best explanation we have for this dynamic:

And "don't sin by letting anger control you." Don't let the sun go down while you are still angry, for anger gives a foothold to the devil. (Ephesians 4:26–27)

Paul said the sin enters when we allow anger to control us. Holding onto anger into the night and/or the next day allows the Enemy an opportunity to lead us into sin.

Funny how temper has nothing to do with age, background, race, physical size, income, or any of the things we might see as differentiators among men. Most issues of unforgiveness in men actually begin with anger. Even when we get hurt, anger can be connected to the offense.

And do not grieve the Holy Spirit of God, with whom you were sealed for the day of redemption. Get rid of all bitterness, rage and anger, brawling and slander, along with every form of malice. Be kind and compassionate to one another, forgiving each other, just as in Christ God forgave you. (Ephesians 4:30–32 NIV)

When Jesus has sacrificed everything to forgive us for all our sin and then we choose to not forgive someone, we cause grief, sadness, and sorrow for the Holy Spirit. When we choose death (unforgiveness) over life (forgiveness), the emotion God feels toward us is associated with what we feel when someone dies.

Let's take a look at the first three sins that Paul tells us to "get rid of."

- Bitterness

The word itself suggests a root that can produce the fruit of hatred. As a bitter fruit will produce a bad taste in the mouth and even cause someone to spit it out, hatred produces a bitter quality in our lives. Anger is the root that when not pulled out eventually produces bitterness and, in full bloom, becomes hatred.

- Rage

Rage is a sudden outburst fueled by anger. When someone flies into a rage, we always know that anger is the original source of the behavior. A man enraged is overcome by anger controlling him. This can be likened to a lit fuse on a bomb. Anger-sssssssssssssssssssss-rage! Rage is an emotional explosion of anger.

A man who has a constant tendency toward fits of rage also has a long list of unresolved anger issues in his heart. His fuse stays lit. That is why explosions happen so quickly for him. Anything that he deems upsetting can create a detonation of extreme anger.

- Anger

When the motivation for anger is righteousness and justice, there is no sin, as we just stated. Anger can be a justified emotion when the object is focused on the unrighteous actions of people, not the people themselves. This reminds us of the old saying: Hate the sin, not the sinner.

But let's get real: being angry only for righteousness' sake is a tough one. The majority of our anger is connected to sin. In the Gospels of Matthew (21:12–13), Mark (11:15–17), and John (2:14–16), Jesus' anger in the temple is documented. But he hurt no one. He attacked no one. He only turned over their tables and drove them out. He stopped their behavior. He cursed no one, but quoted Scripture about the intention of God's house. This concept teaches us an angry jealousy for the glory of God, not promoting anyone's self-interests.

The anger Paul speaks of in verse 31 leads to sin. When anger is unrighteous and remains, we leave the door wide open for Satan. A snake cannot crawl in through a closed door, but give him just a small crack and he will slither in every time.

Self-Centered Anger

Years ago while teaching and discipling men, I prayed that God would show me a way to explain the difference between anger that goes the right way and then the wrong way, the difference between God's way and man's way. How could I explain the difference between verse 26 and verse 31? Here is the progression with both paths beginning at the same place—anger.

Self-Centered Progression of Anger

Anger

Grudge

Bitterness

Hatred

- How can you know when your anger has become a grudge?

A grudge is when someone's name is mentioned or you think of that person and immediately you feel anger, as if the issue happened yesterday. A grudge keeps anger fresh and current. If someone says a person's name and you feel you have to "play your tape" about how bad he/she is or how much you do not like the person, that is a grudge.

- How can you know when your grudge has turned into bitterness?

For most people, at the grudge stage you will still consider getting things straight. You are angry but willing to reconcile. Bitterness takes reconciliation off the table. You are no longer willing to make things right. Aristotle defined bitterness as "the resentful spirit that refuses reconciliation."[4] To apply our earlier analogy, you have taken the person hostage in your heart.

- How can you know when your bitterness has turned to hatred?

A major indicator of hatred is when someone wants to remove a person completely out of his/her life. In fact, the personal cost of seeing their removal will slowly become a lower and lower consideration. This is exactly why, for any law enforcement agency, hatred is such a strong motive for murder. The desire to be rid of the person causes the murderer to lose respect for life.

Ironically, the hater devalues himself as well. He will jeopardize his own life to take action against the other person. One of the games the Enemy plays here is to convince the hater that physically eliminating the person will actually take care of their problem and life can return to normal. Of course, that only brings devastation to everyone involved.

This can also be a motivation for suicide, when self-hate overtakes all reasoning. Eliminating the problem actually means eliminating yourself.

There are times when a man is filled with hatred regarding a number of situations in his life, but feels powerless to act with those he hates. That is why there is suddenly a shooting involving innocent people, a fight in a crowded room of strangers, a road-rage incident, or a violent exchange with a police officer. The out-of-control feelings of anger fly like gas fumes through a funnel to a fire, igniting a horrible explosion of rage. Unresolved and misdirected anger coming out at the wrong place at the wrong time is most often a product of growing hatred.

If you know you have an anger issue on *any* of these levels, please get help before there is a tragedy down the road. When we see the news about a shooter who no one suspected, you can bet the majority of the time, even he would have never thought he could do such a thing just a few years, maybe even months, prior to the event.

For some of you, there may be a relationship (or relationships) in your life where you just realized you are in one of the four stages—anger, grudge, bitterness, or hatred. Did looking at the progression and definitions make you realize you are deeper into anger than you suspected? No matter who the issue is with, please take the necessary steps to make things right before you move to a deeper state.

One truth I know for certain: when we find ourselves consistently in the grudge stage with people or struggling with ongoing bitterness, the state of our mind and heart will affect our purity and our truth. Why? Because our motives stay tainted. Our heart is haunted by constant bitterness, choosing death over life with no end in sight.

Wouldn't this be a great time to get things right? Why is today not the perfect time to seek forgiveness or grant forgiveness? There is certainly no coincidence you are reading this and you have been convicted of a relationship that needs reconciliation.

Remember—how the other person responds does not matter at all. God only holds you responsible for your part.

If it is possible, as far as it depends on you, live at peace with everyone. (Romans 12:18 NIV)

Look at Paul's qualifiers here: If it is possible and as far as it depends on you. In short, for peace, all you can do is all you can do.

The Enemy wants us to believe that if we let our anger go and release forgiveness toward the person, then that resolve makes them "win" and us "lose." He tells us that forgiveness is a loss. Yet again, no matter how that may feel, it is a lie.

There are times when talking through forgiveness and getting rid of bitterness and hatred are best done when we have help. Talking to a pastor, counselor, or a trusted Christian friend to work through the issues is sometimes the best decision because an issue is very hurtful and traumatic. Prayer and accountability are also important tools to health and restoring truth in our lives.

Then Peter came to him and asked, "Lord, how often should I forgive someone who sins against me? Seven times?" "No, not seven times," Jesus replied, "but seventy times seven! (Matthew 18:21–22)

Jesus was not teaching the disciples that on the four-hundred-and-ninety-first time someone offends that you can then take action against the offender. Peter thought seven times was a huge display of grace, but Jesus corrected his math.

The idea here is that you forgive so much that you stop counting. Who would actually keep count of wrongs into the hundreds? Another way of interpreting this passage is: Don't keep score, just like God doesn't with us. When you apply Jesus' answer to the context of all New Testament teaching, we must forgive others as often and to the same degree as God forgives us.

Do you see how the purity that we discussed in the first part of the book is strongly connected to truth in our lives? The two qualities must unite and become one in us. Each flows into the other, like a great marriage.

God-Centered Anger

Let's go back to revisit Ephesians 4:30–32. Paul is communicating that he wants the Christians at Ephesus to have a total abstinence of evil. As with Jesus' definition of adultery, it's more than just *not* practicing evil, but not even *thinking* about evil, not allowing evil of any kind to take root in our hearts to open the door to the Enemy.

Let's look at the three commands Paul gives in verse 32.

Be kind and compassionate to one another, forgiving each other, just as in Christ God forgave you. (NIV)

- Kind

Kindness is love in practical action. There are three ways we experience kindness from a person: countenance—the reflection of the heart on the face; words—speaking proactive encouragement and gentleness; and actions—doing kind things, expressing love.

- Compassionate

Compassion in the heart is the motive for being kind and applying love in practical action. Compassion is the root and kindness is the fruit. These two walk hand-in-hand. When do we ever see one without the other?

- Forgiving

Whenever you make a practice of forgiveness and dealing graciously with people, then you can be consistent in expressing compassion and committing to acts of kindness. There is a progression to these three qualities where they stand alone yet also work together in a Christlike synergy.

When you take the definitions we have applied to the three sins of anger, rage, and bitterness and the three virtues of compassion, kindness, and forgiveness, we find something very interesting. Because Paul was an articulate genius, his application and coordination of topics such as this is often found in his teaching and writing.

- Anger — Compassion
- Rage — Kindness
- Bitterness — Forgiveness

The sins stand in contrast to the virtues. Compassion cannot be expressed in anger. Kindness cannot be expressed when rage is present. Forgiveness cannot occur without letting go of bitterness. The ultimate point of ridding ourselves of these three sins and practicing the three virtues is both defense and offense. We not only stop ourselves from words and actions that hurt others and ourselves, but we can be proactive in representing Christ and promoting His kingdom.

Finally, we see that the reason we can live this new life is because God in Christ has forgiven us. Thus far, we have been dealing with aspects of self-centered anger. For clarity, before we move on, here is the cycle once again:

Anger

Grudge

Bitterness

Hatred

But when we allow God to have our anger, this is the new progression:

<u>God-Centered Progression of Anger</u>

Anger

Resolve

Forgiveness

Love

Both patterns begin with the *same* emotion and response—anger. But when taken away from our flesh and given to God, things turn positive quickly. When we sin, what does God immediately desire and seek with us? Resolve. So should we with others.

Earlier we said that resolve is still an option in the grudge stage. That is the key turning point and crossroads. So if we will choose resolve, then a grudge never occurs, so bitterness never takes root and hatred is completely off the table.

Many years ago, I found a fascinating news story about Chris Carrier of Coral Gables, Florida. In 1974, when he was ten years old, a man who was angry with his father abducted Chris. The kidnapper tortured and burned him with lit cigarettes, stabbed him numerous times with an ice pick, shot him in the head, and then dumped him out to die in the Everglades. (Yes, the place with the highest population of gators and pythons in the country.) But somehow, Chris miraculously survived and managed to get to a nearby road where he was found. His only lasting physical effect from the ordeal was losing sight in one eye. His attacker was never captured.

Chris later began a relationship with Christ and eventually became a youth pastor at a church in Florida. One day, he received word from authorities that a man named David McAllister, a seventy-seven-year-old frail and blind ex-con living in a Miami Beach nursing home, had confessed to committing the crime all those years ago.

Right away, Chris headed to Miami. Did he take a gun? Did he plot revenge on the way there? After all, now the tables were turned. The old man was helpless, just as Chris had been when McAllister tortured, stabbed, shot, and left him for dead. But no, revenge was not Chris's motive as had been his captor's. Chris was going God's direction toward resolve and forgiveness—and, amazingly, yes, even love.

Chris began visiting McAllister regularly, reading the Bible to him and praying for him. Through these visits, Chris led McAllister to the Lord of redemption and restoration. Chris said, "While many people can't understand how I could forgive David McAllister, from my point of view, I couldn't *not* forgive him. If I'd chosen to hate him all these years, or spent my life looking for revenge, then I wouldn't be the man I am today, the man my wife and children love, the man God has helped me to be."

And get this: McAllister told one reporter that Chris was the best friend he had ever had.[5]

We cannot explain the outcome of a story such as this without the power of Christ and His teachings. But to experience the many miracles that he did, Chris Carrier had to *choose* to obey Jesus. And his last line says it all: "the man God has helped me to *be*."

Maybe you have had something just as evil happen to you in your life. Or maybe anywhere you are holding onto bitterness pales in comparison to Chris's story. Regardless of being equal to or less than, the application remains the same.

The same miracle is available.

The same grace is available.

The same freedom is available.

Chapter Eleven

Ten Steps to Truth

Truth stands the test of time; lies are soon exposed.
—Proverbs 12:19 TLB

For this final chapter of part two, I want to give you ten practical principles to help you apply truth in your life.

1. Make a list of people you need to forgive.

Schedule some dedicated time in a quiet spot without your phone or other distractions. Ask God for guidance and begin to write down the names that come to mind. The importance of staying in a state of prayer is to allow God to show you anyone with whom you may have a bigger issue than you realize. Or possibly even someone with whom you still have an issue but thought you had forgotten about or let go.

Once you are confident you have a complete list, tell God how you feel about each person and situation. Talk to Him about *why* you feel the way you do. Tell Him how you believe you were wronged. He can handle your blunt honesty, as is made clear by David's prayers in Psalms.

Next, ask Him what to do about each person on your list. Do what He tells you. Generally, He will give you two choices. The first is to forgive the person while giving your anger to God. There are times when personal interaction is not possible or somehow not best for the situation. The second is to go to the person, if you can. You may need to talk over the issues. You may simply need to grant or ask for forgiveness and you do not require anything from them. If the person has died, if possible, go to the gravesite, talk out loud, and then leave your issue and anger there. While this might sound strange, many who have practiced this graveside forgiveness have come away with genuine release.

For serious and deep offenses, you may need to get accountability from a brother and/or guidance from a pastor or counselor. The bottom line here is to do as Paul commanded and get rid of your anger, grudge, bitterness, and hatred.

2.   Once you take care of your list, keep the list short.

Paul stated to "not let the sun go down on your anger." The next time you feel offended, get things resolved quickly. You or the other person may need to allow time to process or cool down, but as soon as possible, work it out. I once heard a Bible teacher say, "You can measure your maturity level as a Christian by the length of time between an offense and your attempt to resolve." Maturity leads to quick forgiveness. Immaturity creates denial or ignoring the problem, which, of course, creates a new issue. Wouldn't it feel good to keep your list constantly clean and never let it build up again? Continual accountability with a couple of brothers is a great way to keep your list short.

Stay humble and apologize quickly. Do not create a standoff, waiting out the other person to resolve first. The faster you get it right, the less time there is for things to go *more* wrong.

Face-to-face verbal communication is always best. Talking on the phone is the second preference. Texts and emails are too often misread, misinterpreted, and misunderstood, and can actually create new problems. Avoid those methods unless it is the *only* means available.

3. Develop a set of truth principles.

A principle is a self-directed guideline you create and follow on your own for personal growth and protection. Here is a personal example for me: If I speak something out loud about someone else, positive or negative, I need to either have already said it to the person or plan on telling them the next possible opportunity. Whether a compliment or a criticism, I never want for them to hear my words secondhand. If you do need to vent first to a trusted friend for perspective, just agree with yourself that the other person will be next.

If we make a practice of moving from gossip to accountability by going directly to people, this can sometimes, unfortunately, create some enemies along the way. Lots of people,

Christian or not, do not like people who speak the truth or want to resolve in truth. Denial is always easier than facing up to an issue.

Here is the story that created the principle example I gave you: Many years ago a friend recommended I begin to work with a certain businessman. I called and left a message. No response. I emailed. No response. I tried calling again. Nothing. Finally, several days later, I sent an email to my friend about the lack of response and how the guy was not going to stay in business very long... *gripe, gripe, gripe.*

Well, my busy, cut-to-the-chase friend just hit forward on the email and sent it straight to the person. Within a few hours, the front desk buzzed me that the guy was on the line. I suspected I could be met with some *hostility.* But no, there was *humility.*

The man profusely apologized and said he was out and unavailable because of a death in his family. To be honest, I am not sure if I heard another word he said after that. I was humbled in a major way and vowed that day that I would never do anything like that again. That event forever changed my communication ethics and standards. That point brings us to number four.

4. Let your yes be yes and your no be no.

"Just say a simple, 'Yes, I will,' or 'No, I won't.' Anything beyond this is from the evil one." (Matthew 5:37)

And since you know that he cares, let your language show it. Don't add words like "I swear to God" to your own words. Don't show your impatience by concocting oaths to hurry up God. Just say yes or no. Just say what is true. That way, your language can't be used against you. (James 5:12 MSG)

We should aspire to be men with a reputation for making concise and firm decisions. No fear, blame, or deflection to a just-in-case-plan-B. We should be counter-cultural and make solid, biblical decisions. Then take the hit if it is wrong and be humble if it is right.

5. Attitude and tone are just as crucial as your words.

I learned this one the hard way many years ago when my wife started saying, "It's not *what* you say but *how* you say it." (When I share this principle in my men's conference, I always pause after "It's not what you say but . . . " and the men always finish the phrase in unison. Evidently, I am not the only guy with this issue.)

I can say the right thing the wrong way and then the right thing is never heard, because how I said it overshadowed what I said! This comes from me being too intense at times. When I was young and would tell my dad that someone at school called me little, he would smile and say, "Son, tell them you're not little, you're just wound tight." (Man, that is still true.)

For twenty years I managed a large nonprofit ministry. There were years when I had up to fifty-plus employees to oversee in five different areas. One particular time a young man asked me if he could take off on the upcoming Friday to help his parents move. I paused, ran through some other people's schedules in my mind for a moment, and then told him he could take off.

Sometime the next week, I realized he had been at work that previous Friday. I went to see what happened, asking if his parents weren't able to move that day. He answered, "No, they moved." Now puzzled, I asked, "How come you didn't help?" He said, "Well, I could just tell when I asked you if I could take off that you didn't really want me to be gone." When I asked him if I had said he could take the day off, he replied, "Yes, but it wasn't what you said, it was how you said it." I was crushed. Another lesson learned in verbal *and* nonverbal communication. I am convinced as people we *read* one another far more than we *listen*.

6. Our words either attract people to Christ or distract people from Christ.

Let's start with distraction. Rude, vulgar, crass, racial, and sexist remarks have no place in a Christ follower's language. Particularly when others have little to no context of us, they assume our speech is a 100 percent complete reflection of our heart.

These people are as useless as dried-up springs or as mist blown away by the wind. They are doomed to blackest darkness. They brag about themselves with empty, foolish boasting. With an appeal to twisted sexual desires, they lure back into sin those who have barely escaped from a lifestyle of deception. They promise freedom, but they themselves are slaves of sin and corruption. For you are a slave to whatever controls you. And when people escape from the wickedness of the world by knowing our Lord and Savior Jesus Christ and then get tangled up and enslaved by sin again, they are worse off than before. (2 Peter 2:17–20)

Now for attraction: *When you talk, you should always be kind and pleasant so you will be able to answer everyone in the way you should. (Colossians 4:6 NCV)*

When might someone talk to you about your faith? Anytime.

Who should we be ready to answer? Everyone.

When should we be ready and able to answer? Always.

How should we speak? With pleasant kindness.

7. Men who follow Christ are not silent men.

I said silent, not quiet. There is a difference. A lot of men do not have to worry about saying too much or too little, because you are just not going to hear from them at all. But silence has hurt just as many people as words have. Sometimes it is not *what* we say, but what we *do not* say.

The lips of the wise give good advice; the heart of a fool has none to give. (Proverbs 15:7)

The wise are known for their understanding, and pleasant words are persuasive. (Proverbs 16:21)

Many of us have experienced anguish in our lives from a father who never said, "I love you," "I'm proud of you," or "That's my boy." We cannot repeat that same anguish by not saying what we need to say. We cannot be guilty of perpetuating, "Well, she knows I love her," or "My son knows I love him. He knows men don't have to say it."

The majority of the time, silence from men boils down to pride. How ironic that the English word *pride* has a big ol' *I* right in the middle. If a man is sitting back being quiet when he needs to speak, the reason is either pride or fear. So often fear is based on not looking bad in the moment, which is really just disguised pride.

8. We provoke our own response.

A gentle answer turns away wrath, but a harsh word stirs up anger. (Proverbs 15:1 NIV)

A gentle response defuses anger, but a sharp tongue kindles a temper-fire. (Proverbs 15:1 MSG)

Have you ever had a day when you keep thinking, *Why is everybody being such a jerk?* Or this: *All I did was ask a simple question and I got my head bit off!* The next simple question is how did you ask that simple question? How we speak is very often how we are spoken to.

One of the best rules of communication I have ever heard was the fact that we *train* others how to listen and respond to us by how we listen and respond to them. We have to carefully listen to ourselves speak as well as others.

9. Be an encourager.

Our culture is increasingly demeaning and mean, with the anonymous online community leading the way. If you have been employed on the Cut-Down Demolition Crew, it is high time to just quit. The benefits are lousy anyway. Join the Courageous Construction Company and begin building people up. They will feel better. You will feel better. You will be a better man. Use your words for building bridges, not burning them.

I want to challenge you to an experiment: Choose a day and work hard to only encourage people, allowing nothing else to come out of your mouth. Just one day. But here is the added touch: Figure out how to encourage *everyone* with whom you communicate—the convenience-store clerk, barista, waiter, coworker, boss, wife, child, everyone. See if you don't feel good about making people feel good.

The word *encourage* means "to place courage in." Choose to put courage in those you encounter because the God of courage is alive in you.

So encourage each other and build each other up, just as you are already doing. (1 Thessalonians 5:11)

10. Be an active listener.

Concentrate on what the other person is saying, not on what you are going to say next. Try to understand where the other person is coming from, not on how to get them to see your point.

Ask for clarification on anything you do not understand. Recap your perspective of what you heard. This is to ensure the other person that you understood them and allow for correction of anything misunderstood.

Take initiative in reaching the truth. Be proactive in communication. Decide to major in the art of listening.

Fools think their own way is right, but the wise listen to others. (Proverbs 12:15)

Truth + Love

Then we will no longer be immature like children. We won't be tossed and blown about by every wind of new teaching. We will not be influenced when people try to trick us with lies so clever they sound like the truth. Instead, we will speak the truth in love, growing in every way more and more like Christ, who is the head of his body, the church. (Ephesians 4:14–15)

A way to translate Paul's phrase "speak the truth in love" is "truthing in love," meaning our words and actions are continually mixing truth with love, love with truth. We work to balance the two as Christ did. Our beliefs match our actions. Actions match beliefs. Your life is marked by truthing love and loving truth. What we say, we do. What we do, we say.

For us as men, there are times that truth in love means a hug and other times a swift kick in the pants. As brothers in Christ, we have to be able to give each other both and know when we need which. That is what accountability truly is.

Jesus boldly proclaimed truth while also boldly loving people. He was killed on a cross for doing both. His love drove His truth and His truth drove His love. That is our hope and goal with His life in us.

I want to leave you with some questions to consider. If you gave total control of your mouth, your tongue, and your speech to Christ right now:

- Who would be apologized to that was not before?

- What relationship would be made right?

- Who would be thanked that never had been before?

- Who would be told they are loved and appreciated that had not before?

- Who would be encouraged that either was discouraged before or left to silence?

- Who would see and hear Christ in you like never before?

Part Three

Believing,

Becoming,

Being

a Man of Righteousness

(Righting Wrongs)

Chapter Twelve

Called to the Dance

Then the LORD God said,
"It is not good for the man to be alone.
I will make a helper who is just right for him."
Then the LORD God . . . brought her to the man. "
At last!" the man exclaimed.
—Genesis 2:18, 22–23

For most men, marriage is going to be a major element and dynamic of life. Whether you have been married for four years or forty years, whether you are on your first or third, whether you feel like your relationship has been successful or a failure, one thing we can all agree on: marriage takes work. Put two sinners of different genders in the same house and sooner or later sparks are going to fly.

If you are single or single again I want to encourage you to walk through the content in this chapter carefully to invest in your future. I had one young man go through my resources just because he felt he needed to deepen in his walk with the Lord as a man. Two weeks after he finished, he met his bride. When he went through this material on marriage, he was just hoping to use it one day. His reasoning was great, but God had something far bigger in store for him. As they say, timing is everything.

She saw that the tree was beautiful and its fruit looked delicious, and she wanted the wisdom it would give her. So she took some of the fruit and ate it. Then she gave some to her husband, who was with her, and he ate it, too. (Genesis 3:6)

As we see in Genesis 3, Adam let God and Eve down in the garden when he chose to eat the fruit with her, instead of defending his bride and himself as his Father had prepared him to do. Because of inheriting Adam's passive nature, one of our greatest struggles in marriage is the art of leading. Yes, leading a woman and a family is an art, not a science.

The proof is watching a guy attempt to apply all the same approaches to his second wife as he did his first. Funny how a man starts to think the problem is with women, when the rule of insanity applies to him: to keep doing the same thing while hoping for a different outcome. The same goes for trying to apply an identical approach to raising a girl as to a boy or the second child opposed to the first. Another reason I call this art is because marriage and parenting are beautiful when someone knows what they are doing and really ugly when they do not.

Manning Up

Financial problems, sexual issues, career conflicts, and communication breakdown all typically stem from leadership problems. In the dysfunction department, there tends to be two overarching issues.

The first is very common: The husband is not leading, so the wife does. Very often everyone around this man sees the dynamic except him because he is in denial.

- The primary reason why a woman leads a family is laziness of the husband.

When I was a pastor, I was visiting with a couple dealing with several major issues. In front of him, I asked her what is one thing you would like to ask of your husband, not a list, just one thing. I will never forget her answer: "I need him to man up!" When I asked her why, she answered, "Because I am so tired of leading."

What causes us as men to not take the role that God gave us at the marriage altar?

Being a first-generation Christ follower has been challenging and difficult for me. One of the biggest reasons is because I have had no pattern to follow. But then the ironic advantage is, well, I have had no pattern to follow. I have been forced my entire life to rely on Scripture and prayer to try to lead a family. As a result, I do not look around and wait for someone to join me, because there has been no one to join me before. I have no choice but to try to lead, because there is no one ahead of me to follow!

I have made a lot of mistakes, a *lot* of mistakes. I have dropped the ball. I have quit, given up, taken a break, slacked off, and questioned why and how I should lead. But I always have to come back to the God-given place of picking myself back up, dusting myself off, and stepping back out in front of my family, asking them for forgiveness, and moving on. But regardless of how godly any family may have been for a man growing up, there is obviously no guarantee the next generation will produce a family leader. It is a personal choice for every man in each generation. You can inherit some amazing qualities, but that does not guarantee application.

Regardless of family history, my responsibility is to have that legacy begin with me. We had two boys who are now adult men. Frankly, when they were growing up, they did not care that I had no example. They just wanted me to lead and show them how to lead. So I have the opportunity through them to double the family legacy, and then if each of them has two children, well, then generations are radically changed.

Imagine someone doing a genealogy study of your family and when the tree arrives at you, they respond, "Whoa! What happened here? A huge shift in the right direction." So what steps can you take to man up and lead when you have never led or haven't in a long time?

First, communicate with God. Give Him your laziness, disobedience, and ignoring your duty as a man who follows Christ. The great news is there is not a single man in history whom God has not forgiven when He has been asked. The other good news is that He can lead your family through you. Just submit to Him. So you lead by following the Head of all families. If you mess up, 'fess up. He will forgive. You can complicate it if you want, but that is how it works—every time.

Second, communicate with your wife. Ask her to forgive you of the same things you asked God to forgive you for. But you should add the fact that you have not loved her to the level she has needed. Leading your wife is loving your wife. Loving your wife is leading your wife. Explain to her any emotions you feel, like being concerned, afraid, and intimidated, but that you really want to change and take your God-given role. Explain that she has done nothing wrong, but your lack of action has put a burden on her she should not have had. You want to free her up to be the best wife, mother, friend, and woman she can be. Most women are so grateful that God has answered their prayers that this will not be a difficult conversation. If you are humble, she will be helpful. If you are repentant, she will resolve.

Third, depending on your circumstances and the ages of your kids, you may have to communicate with them too. You do not have to make a long speech. Just explain that they may notice some changes in how mom and dad do things. Tell them if they have any questions or do not understand something, to just ask. Explain that there may be some different spiritual aspects at home, but you need them to cut you some slack and be patient. Tell them that you are going to work hard to be more consistent and that they need to understand the changes are going to be best for everyone. Tell them that you are really wanting to be the best husband and dad you can, and that you want mom to be happy and for them to be happy. That is what this is all about.

- The second reason why a woman leads a family is the man's fear of his wife.

First, there should be a healthy fear in all our major relationships in the sense that we do not want to disappoint or burden anyone. Respect may be a better word, but this is the same concept as having a fear of God, a deep awe of the position He has in your life. Fear and respect to want to please one another in a marriage is necessary for us to consistently make the right choices for the relationship.

Having an unhealthy fear, especially in today's culture, is rampant. Many men will know this to be true, yet live in denial. I have seen guys as big as NFL linebackers in constant fear of their five-feet-two, one-hundred-ten-pound wife. From my experience, most of us men battle this issue on some level, but pride keeps us from admitting it.

For many men, the discouragement of having failed in the past or the gripping thought of failing in the future often creates paralyzing fear, even if he only *feels* like he has. Regardless, chronic fear is unhealthy. Any husband who is "walking on eggshells" with his wife cannot possibly love her to the full or be happily married. If when your wife says, "We need to talk," you feel like throwing up, that is a good sign you are on shaky ground.

As men, we understand respecting someone and honoring their position without being afraid of them. For example, there is a big difference between a son who obeys dad because he is afraid of the consequences and a son who obeys dad because he so deeply respects him. We understand that concept from bosses to teammates. When we fear our wives, we are not honoring them.

Confession, prayer, and accountability are the best tools to rid us of fear and encourage us to respect our wives in a healthy manner. Talking through this issue with a few brothers may be really difficult, but getting the problem outside of us can bring freedom and change. Most guys in small groups will not have the same marital issues, but they will have areas that need to be discussed and changed. Consistent prayer for grace, strength, and wisdom will help us grow. Last, being accountable for our words and actions with our wives can change the dynamics in our marriages faster than any other method of action.

Now, here is the other side of the coin.

There are men who rule with an iron fist and their wives are fearful, jumpy, and stressed out by their husbands. This is where, in an extreme situation, abuse can begin. But here, I am not talking about physical or verbal abuse, rather simply a man leading his wife and family with a "my way or the highway" approach. This style is out of balance in the other direction from fear. That husband becomes the source of fear. He has to begin to show respect and honor to his wife for her feelings and desires. He must learn to allow for her opinion and value her thoughts, words, and actions. If a man says that doing these things in his marriage is a sign of weakness, my response is that weakness is displayed when a man cannot honor anyone but himself, especially his wife.

Honestly, all of us men tend to lean toward one of these sides—fear of the woman or iron fist of the man. We have a *tendency* toward one or the other and have to work to find balance.

After thirty-five-years-plus in my own marriage and years of meeting and talking with couples of all ages, my humble opinion is the number-one thing a woman wants from her man is security. She is constantly saying in a thousand different ways, "Help me feel loved and safe." And yes, you may have accomplished that yesterday, but now she wants to know if you will do it today too. It is not an event but a lifestyle. For most women, the security bank runs the balance down to zero at the end of each day and the next day needs a fresh deposit. This is not a *detriment*, but God's *design* to teach us how to love unconditionally and sacrificially.

Many men answer the question of "When was the last time you told your wife you love her?" with "She knows I love her" or "Last Valentine's Day." In a healthy, loving marriage, each day needs a fresh supply of security. Of course, we are going to miss and mess up, but when our wives know we are working hard, they will provide grace.

A woman whose husband is afraid of her and refusing to lead is making her feel unloved and insecure. A husband who is ruling with clenched teeth and a closed fist is making her feel unloved and insecure. An insecure woman will never be fulfilled. A smile on her face does not always mean a smile in her heart. My mentor once told me, "You can see the character of a man in his wife's eyes." (Just let that one sink in for a minute.)

The Great Mystery

One of the most abused and mishandled passages of Scripture is Ephesians 5:21–33. Even if you think you know what Paul said, please read every word before moving on to the principle. Focus on your role as a husband. Do not look for what he tells your wife to do, but what he says to you.

And further, submit to one another out of reverence for Christ. For wives, this means submit to your husbands as to the Lord. For a husband is the head of his wife as Christ is the head of the church. He is the Savior of his body, the church. As the church submits to Christ, so you wives should submit to your husbands in everything.

For husbands, this means love your wives, just as Christ loved the church. He gave up his life for her to make her holy and clean, washed by the cleansing of God's word. He did this to present her to himself as a glorious church without a spot or wrinkle or any other blemish. Instead, she will be holy and without fault. In the same way, husbands ought to love their wives as they love their own bodies. For a man who loves his wife actually shows love for himself. No one hates his own body but feeds and cares for it, just as Christ cares for the church. And we are members of his body.

As the Scriptures say, "A man leaves his father and mother and is joined to his wife, and the two are united into one." This is a great mystery, but it is an illustration of the way Christ and the church are one. So again I say, each man must love his wife as he loves himself, and the wife must respect her husband.

The very first thing Paul talks about is a *mutual* submission with clear roles. This passage is often interpreted as subtraction from each other when it is actually addition to one another, division between us when it is really about multiplication of the relationship.

Years ago as I began to be asked to officiate marriage ceremonies and my wife and I were asked to provide premarital counseling, I searched desperately for a way to communicate this passage in the correct manner for optimum understanding. I wanted to help young couples grasp the delicate balance of *mutual* submission in a culture that increasingly rejects and defies the biblical model simply because they do not properly understand what is being stated.

So I asked God to give me a picture, an analogy that I could share with couples that would make sense to them and override the cultural stigma. Here is what I heard Him say very clearly: "Ballroom dancing." My first response was, "Say what?" Then came the connected teaching as He gave me a modern parable.

Picture a large, darkened ballroom dance floor. The spotlight hits the middle of the wood and a couple strolls out to the center. The man is in his tux with tails and black shiny shoes. The woman is in a beautiful, flowing, floor-length gown. They look incredible and you can sense their confidence and strength.

They clasp hands and embrace, and as the music starts, they begin their dance. They hover all around the floor with style and grace, giving the appearance of literally floating as the spotlight follows their every move. They make their work of art look effortless, both beaming and savoring the experience. The two are having fun and proud of what they have mastered in their skill and are now accomplishing together. The packed house looks on with amazement and cannot take their eyes off them. The beautiful sight has everyone mesmerized by this two-become-one experience.

Now, at any point in the dance, does anyone watching them ask, "So, I'm confused. Who's leading?" No. In ballroom dancing, *everyone* knows the man leads and the woman is following his moves. But when a couple is great at this style of dancing, you cannot tell who is leading. If both do what they are supposed to do, you are so taken by their corporate effort that you are not concerned or distracted by who is leading or following. It does not matter to anyone, because what is on display is so beautiful; the art of mutual submission.

But if the man should decide he is tired of leading and stops, what happens? If the woman decides she is sick of following him, what happens? You got it. Not so pretty anymore. Suddenly those watching begin to concern themselves with the issue of who is at fault and what has gone wrong. Roles that were respected and clear become conflicting and confused.

Herein lies a major element in ballroom dancing: The men are taught that the entire point of the dance is to showcase the beauty of the woman with respect, honor, and chivalry.

This picture I have painted for you is the heart of Paul's teaching in Ephesians 5 and also the heart of Jesus for His bride as verse 27 states: *"He did this to present her to himself as a glorious church without a spot or wrinkle or any other blemish. Instead, she will be holy and without fault."*

Die to Yourself

So to get your own dance with your wife right, do you need to get rid of some fear and sweep up some eggshells? Open your fist and hold your wife's hand? As a follower of Jesus, He is both the Example and the Goal.

We must continually ask:

- How would Jesus treat my wife differently than I do?

- What do I think He would want me to change?

- In what areas of my marriage would He affirm me?

I can recall many times when my wife and I were sitting with young couples only weeks away from their wedding day talking about this passage. I looked at the soon-to-be bride and said, "So your role to your husband will be to live for him." Every time, the soon-to-be groom would light up. He looked at me like I had just told him he could live in Hawaii for free. The goofy grin that washed over his face said, "Oh boy! Thanks, sir! That is so awesome! I love you so much for telling her that!"

But then I looked at him and said, "The Bible is also clear on your role. While she is to live for you, you must die for her. Daily. Put her first always. Be willing to place your own wants and wishes aside and always do what is best for your bride. Just as Christ did and does for His bride. Every day, die to yourself. For Christ and the bride He has given you."

Every time, his facial expression changed. He would swallow hard and his eyes said, "Well, we ain't moving to Hawaii after all. . . . Die, huh?" But for the ones truly committed to Jesus, when the idea sunk in, they knew it was right. A look of honor swept over his countenance. Being a Christ-centered husband is a calling from God Himself, with your wife and your marriage being a gift from Him.

Gentlemen, one thing is abundantly clear in Scripture—as a man who follows Christ, life is not about us. We put God first, then our families second. That is how we love Him and them. That is the best way for God to change the world through us!

Chapter Thirteen

The Buck Stops Here

So each generation should set its hope anew on God,
not forgetting his glorious miracles
and obeying his commands.
—Psalm 78:7

The biggest gift we can give our kids is to get ourselves right with God and healthy in spirit, and then get our marriage right and healthy as well. Nothing blesses or burdens our children like the relationship between mom and dad. The health of our marriage often determines the health of our children, because they are a constant reflection of their parents.

For many years as our guys were growing up, we had this saying on our fridge: "Don't allow anything into your own life that you do not want reproduced in your children's lives." While the quote sounds like one from James Dobson, I do not know the source. The idea being that those things we may be able to handle in moderation, our children may commit in excess. We must think this concept through and decide as parents *any* risks that are worth exposing to our children.

Let's go back and revisit our lazy-man/iron-fist examples from the previous chapter. The majority of the time that a man rules his home with an iron fist, he is exasperating his children, while the man who is lazy and afraid of leadership is also lazy in his discipline and often somewhat afraid of his kids too.

The iron-fist man cares about the rules, not the relationship, while the lazy man cares about the relationship and not the rules. Most lazy men want their kids to be their buddies to create less conflict, thus less work.

Kids need parents first and then friends. From my personal experience, I am close friends now with both my adult sons because I was dad when they needed me to be. I certainly made some major mistakes as their father and apologized many times over the years, but they know today I did *my* best to be their dad.

A family formula that has been repeated for many years is: "Rules without Relationship equals Rebellion." But I would add the converse: "Relationship with no Rules equals Running (all over you)." The biblical balance is "Relationship with the Right Rules equals Righteousness."

Many years ago I heard James Dobson share this analogy on his radio show: "Children are like the night watchman. They check all the doors, but they really don't want any of them to open." So often these actions are the child's heart asking, "Do you really love me and how much?" As a dad, that simple truth helped me greatly in attempting to interpret my sons' motives and actions as they were growing up. Sometimes a child's behavior is rebellion that requires discipline and sometimes it is a request for your love. The balance and wisdom lies in discerning the difference.

As children get older and make their own choices, of course they can stray from their foundation. Kids raised in godly homes can get off course and live very different than mom and dad. And those who grow up in horrible homes can turn out to be responsible, upright people. That is the exercise of free will that God gives every person. But we all know that the possibilities are far better for the children to walk in health if mom and dad are doing so. The younger you start, the better the opportunity. But as with anything in life, there are no guarantees. Always remember, especially as they get older and independent, your kids have their own will and ability to choose. Prayer for our children will always be the best offensive and defensive weapon we have to fight on their behalf.

I want to share a practical exercise that could help you and your kids monitor where you are as a dad. Obviously, this requires your children be old enough and mature enough to converse on this level. If they are too young right now, plan on applying this down the road. But if you start young, they will get accustomed to this level of communication and it will not be so difficult later.

Sit your children down together. Tell them you are going to ask some questions and you want total honesty. Tell them they will not get in trouble for telling you the truth. You want the truth. (Gird your loins. This can hurt.) In this setting, there will be zero consequences for anything that is said. This is about getting their feelings out and allowing you to know what wrongs you have done or are doing that need to be made right.

There may be some awkward silence, but plow through and stick with it. If you feel that one or more of your kids will do better one-on-one, then tell them you will be glad to speak with him/her alone after everyone is finished. But some shy children will speak up with the whole family whereas they will not when alone. Regardless, it is important to have the corporate meeting first. There is power for them in numbers, even if there is only two. These meetings will get easier over time and hopefully make all communication better. It also gives your kids a voice inside the family. And honestly, too many families never provide an outlet for the children to speak up and share real feelings until one day when they are in a counselor's office. Maybe this effort could head those days off?

Ask your children these questions:

- Tell me one thing that you believe I am doing right as a dad.

- Tell me one thing that you would like for me to stop or to change.

- Tell me one thing you need from me or want me to do for you.

- Tell me one way I can improve my relationship with you.

Feel free to customize your own questions. You get the idea. Realize that not too many dads sit down with their kids and ask for feedback, so you will be above the norm. Also, when they see you are serious about improving as a dad to this level, it communicates a great deal of care and validation of their feelings. Last, wouldn't you rather know exactly how they feel and deal with it, so you can be the best dad and the best example of Jesus you can be? As a father who follows Christ, job one is showing them the closest thing to their heavenly Father that you can.

Of course, you can also apply this anytime to your individual kids, but the family dynamic is important to deal with first.

You Can't Go Home Again

The toughest place in our lives to get things straight as adults can be inside the families in which we grew up, because the issues have been around for so long. Family patterns may have been in place for decades with no change and no desire to change. There could have been an "elephant in the room" for a long time because no one wants to bring up the issues. This is where many men learn the dysfunction of denial, where our own issues began and then grew up with us. Even still, for us to truly lead our own families in health, we must do all we can to make relationships right in the family in which we grew up. Our obedience can break down strongholds of the Enemy that have existed for generations.

- An adult man is no longer dad or mom's little boy.

I am not talking about hugging your dad or letting mom kiss you on the cheek. I am talking about if they still treat you like a child when you are clearly a grown man. Do not play that game anymore, and do not allow them to play it either. This issue can manifest itself in two ways—babying or bullying. Most often dad bullies and mom babies, but the opposite is certainly possible.

Some guys will demand to be treated with a certain level of respect in their career, but then become a little boy again around dad or mom. There are few things a wife can loathe and disrespect more than her husband allowing mom to not recognize the man he is and allowing her to keep enabling the little-boy syndrome. In fact, a lot of wives will at least understand a mother's heart and not blame the mom-in-law as much as her husband. But this can cause great damage to the relationship between a man's mother and his wife. If your wife has a problem with your mom and this is her reasoning, just know your wife is right, you are wrong, and mom needs to be gracefully put in her place. It is a hard talk, but it must happen. If you married someone just like your mom and your wife has continued the babying, it is time to talk to your wife *and* your mom.

Regarding dad, there are two possible dysfunctions here. As with mom, there are dads out there who will baby their sons. Actually it could be classified better as bailing out, rather than babying. That is mostly in the form of rescuing them out of bad situations and not allowing them out from under the parents' protection to experience the real world. In fact, a father bailing out his son can slowly enable bad behavior and choices. We raise our sons to become men, so enabling stunts the growth that God intends for them.

If dad keeps bailing you out, you must talk to him. Level with him. Speak the truth in love. Time to let go and grow. The majority of dads will respect that you stood up and laid the issues on the table. He may even be relieved.

Or maybe you *are* the bailout dad. Talk to your son. It is time to let him grow up. Turn Him over to Christ.

Second, bullying from dad creates a boatload of issues in a male of any age. I have seen grown, powerful men live in fear of their fathers. He may have never even hit his son, but the verbal abuse and intimidation is devastating. Generally, if this behavior begins as a boy, it often continues until the son puts a stop to it. If you are being bullied by dad, sit down with him and communicate to say this has got to stop and why. Ending this dysfunction is going to help the entire family.

If you are the bullying dad, you need to get counseling to uncover where this started, deal with the root, and stop the behavior.

Here is the bottom line to this overall issue: If you feel like you are still just a child—at whatever age—to your father or mother or both, then it is going to be difficult for you to lead your own family. If the two most important people in your development show that they do not believe you have grown up, that is a hindrance to your maturity and confidence.

Go talk to mom and/or dad and get these or any other dysfunctional issues out in the open and straight. Yes, conflict and confrontation are always very hard, but everyone will feel better when the dysfunction ends. And your wife will totally respect you for taking charge of this lethal area. You will also be less likely to repeat this behavior or allow it with your own children by ending the pattern with you.

Here is the great news: God has ordained your marriage and made you and your wife one. If you have children, He has opened the womb of your wife and blessed you to be a father. He obviously believes you can do it and He has validated you. What else do you need if God Himself has given you His approval and authority?

Circles of Influence

A chameleon is an ugly lizard that changes colors depending on his surroundings. As guys, we can be social chameleons. Does your personality change according to your environment? Is the image you portray to friends at work, in the neighborhood, at church, and in social circles all the same guy? Most of us men can be tempted to show different sides of our personalities depending on what we believe the people in the room want to see. So we will change who we are perceived to be to please people and be accepted. But that reflects a clear identity issue.

Are you the funny guy in one room, but the spiritual guy in another room? Are you the quiet guy in this one, but the vulgar guy in that one? Are you the tech-savvy guy over here and the sports guy over there? Get the picture? No matter how guilty we may be of this social shape-shifting, deep in our heart, we do not like it. It just does not feel right. Why? Because God created each of us to be a whole and sole person, not eight versions of someone no one really knows. In trying to please everyone else, we are not being true to who we are.

I am not talking slight shifts in approach due to personality. We all have places we can "let our hair down" and places we are more reserved. I am talking about major swings like an actor playing different roles.

So here is a principle for you: Wherever you are, be the same guy. Do not give people who you think they want. Be who you are in *every* room.

People like knowing what they are going to get from you. Don't make them guess who you are going to be. People will more likely respect you, rather than having to constantly ask, "Who's he going to be this time?" And if someone does not like you? So what. That's their loss.

If God wants someone else in a situation, He will put that person there. If He wants you there, then give them you. If He has ordained you to be in a certain place or position, then He needs *you* there. Be who He made you. If you are good enough for God, then why shouldn't you be good enough for you—and anyone else?

To support this point, look at the life of Jesus in the Gospels. He showed us so many different sides of His personality, yet He was always the definition of consistent. You just cannot imagine the disciples asking, "Wow, I wonder what mood He's going to be in today?" No. Didn't happen. Or "Well, he's tried being funny with the Pharisees, then He tried acting smarter than them. That didn't work, so I wonder what He'll do next?" Nope. Never went down like that. They knew who He was, and the primary reason is He knew who He was and He always presented exactly that! As you mature in Christ, you will find yourself becoming more balanced and more consistent. A definite sign of spiritual maturity is becoming confident in Him and comfortable in who you are. We will find our true identity in a relationship with Christ.

Jesus Christ is the same yesterday, today, and forever. (Hebrews 13:8)

Right now, we are confined on this planet in this world; however, as believers, we also live in God's kingdom. We live in the world, but inside Christ—in His economy, in His protection, in His provision, in His mission, in His calling, in His death, and in His life.

Gentlemen, our job on this earth is to be a force of righteousness to change things into the way God would have them. That starts with us, then our families, then our circles of influence, and into the world. There are wrongs today in our own lives, in our families, in our circles, in the world that God fully intends for us to make right. The only question is, will we?

Our Father in heaven,
Reveal who you are.
Set the world right;
Do what's best—
as above, so below.
(Matthew 6:9–10 MSG)

Chapter Fourteen

Batman & the Me Monster

David replied to the Philistine,
"You come to me with sword, spear, and javelin,
but I come to you in the name of
the Lord of Heaven's Armies
... This is the Lord's battle,
and he will give you to us!"
—1 Samuel 17:45, 47

Anytime I ask a group of men their favorite superhero, a large percentage will answer with "Batman." The answer as to why is always very much the same too. Batman has no super powers. He cannot fly. He is not faster than a locomotive. He does not have super-human strength. But Batman is just so cool.

Here is why a lot of men, including myself, relate to Batman: He had a tormented childhood that led to a dysfunctional adult life with no lasting relationships, except for his butler who is on the payroll. Now that is really sad, isn't it? We actually feel a little sorry for him. When do we ever feel sorry for Superman? We can relate to Batman. Not so much Superman.

But here is the upside for Batman: As Bruce Wayne, he has an apparent unlimited amount of money because he owns a global mega-corporation. Then add the genius-level intelligence. Next throw in the alter ego that fights crime and administers justice—anonymously. What is not to love about that?

But here is a very ironic aspect of Batman I think we as guys get on a subconscious level and why I personally connect with him: He is just a man who has a driving passion to right wrongs, but he has far more success all over Gotham City than he does in his own heart. Doesn't that sound familiar, gentlemen?

As for me, I am not rich. I am not powerful. Smart, maybe, but not intelligent. But I so relate to this dilemma. Conquer the city but fail in my own heart. As guys, we can rescue a situation in a half hour for someone else, but cannot get a handle on a dysfunction of our own for a decade. As the old comic strip character *Pogo* said, "We have met the enemy and he is us!"

Flaws & Faith

The closest person in Scripture to Batman, in my opinion, is David, whom I have frequently brought up in these pages.

The young shepherd boy has been well trained by being left alone for long periods of time with the family's sheep flocks. He has had to fight off bears and lions to keep them from eating the sheep. And himself. As a result of his experience in the field and his deep faith in God, he has gotten to be a really tough, gutsy young man.

David gets sent to the front lines to take food to his brothers. When he arrives, he quickly hears about this giant named Goliath who is taunting the nation and his God. Puzzled as to why everyone is so afraid, he decides to take care of the standoff singlehandedly.

After a brief taunting by Goliath and an exchange of words between he and David, the shepherd-warrior runs at the giant and nails him in the head with a rock. Then he grabs the guy's sword and cuts his head off. Problem solved. The nation saved. God glorified.

No surprise to anyone, David later becomes king. But then after some ongoing success as a conqueror, one spring he decides to stay home while his army ventures out. During a bored afternoon strolling on his roof, he sees a beautiful woman naked, bathing in her courtyard. He stops thinking with his brain and sends for her. Problem started. A nation jeopardized. God ignored.

Later, Bathsheba tells David she is pregnant and she knows the baby is his because her husband has been off at war with the army by the king's very orders. He calls her husband, Uriah, back home for a furloughed weekend to sleep with his wife. Uriah has so much loyalty and integrity that he will not allow himself the luxury and sleeps outside the palace. David gets desperate and sends word back to the generals to arrange Uriah's death on the front lines. Problem worsened.

Yet another example of how we can right the wrongs of a nation, yet fail in our own hearts. Nathan the prophet knew that God wanted to get through to David, so he told the king a story about a guy who owned a pet lamb and how a rich and powerful man took the lamb to offer as a meal to a guest rather than using one from his own flock. David flew into a rage and demanded immediate justice.

Then Nathan said to David, "You are that man! The LORD, the God of Israel, says: I anointed you king of Israel and saved you from the power of Saul. I gave you your master's house and his wives and the kingdoms of Israel and Judah. And if that had not been enough, I would have given you much, much more. Why, then, have you despised the word of the LORD and done this horrible deed?" (2 Samuel 12:7–9)

But here is where David one-ups Batman and shows us the key to taking his belief back into his being.

Have mercy on me, O God, because of your unfailing love. Because of your great compassion, blot out the stain of my sins. Wash me clean from my guilt. Purify me from my sin. For I recognize my rebellion; it haunts me day and night. Against you, and you alone, have I sinned; I have done what is evil in your sight. (Psalm 51:1–4)

He goes deeper and gets proactive about where he knows he needs to go with God:

Restore to me the joy of your salvation, and make me willing to obey you. Then I will teach your ways to rebels, and they will return to you. Forgive me for shedding blood, O God who saves; then I will joyfully sing of your forgiveness. Unseal my lips, O Lord, that my mouth may praise you. (Psalm 51:12–15)

David was now broken, praying, and changing. Inviting God in to do what only He can do when we have seen the worst of what we can do. Understanding that we cannot, but He can. God has to work *on* us, then *in* us, before He can work *through* us. This is what happens when a loving, merciful, persistent, grace-filled God intervenes in the life of a dysfunctional, issue-ridden, self-centered man. Redemption, forgiveness, healing, salvation, and restoration occur. Righteousness meets rebellion and wrongs are made right.

In our world today, where is The Joker, or The Penguin, or Two Face, or even Goliath? The enemies do not seem to be so clearly marked in our battle. Or are they?

There is an old tale of a successful young Wall Street broker who met and fell in love with a rising young actress. He soon decided he wanted to marry her. Needing to be very cautious with his career, he decided that before proposing he should have a private investigator check her out. With his growing wealth and image to maintain, he did not want to make a mistake with the woman he married.

He asked the agency to keep his identity a secret from the detective investigating the actress so his query could never get back to anyone. After several weeks, the investigator completed his report, stating that the actress had a very clean past, a surprisingly spotless reputation, and that her friends, as well as the people with whom she worked, were all reputable—except for one. The report's last sentence read, "The only blemish we can find is that she is often seen around town with a young businessman known for his questionable practices and principles."[6]

This story illustrates well how we often are so thorough in judging other's actions, just like King David, while missing the glaring fact that we have major issues in our own hearts that need to be addressed.

Living Sacrifice?

So how can we be proactive about staying off the roof and not missing our issues?

And so, dear brothers and sisters, I plead with you to give your bodies to God because of all he has done for you. Let them be a living and holy sacrifice—the kind he will find acceptable. This is truly the way to worship him. Don't copy the behavior and customs of this world, but let God transform you into a new person by changing the way you think. Then you will learn to know God's will for you, which is good and pleasing and perfect. (Romans 12:1–2)

How can we be a "sacrifice" and be "living" at the same time? After all, a sacrifice is killed in a display of offering and worship. This is an oxymoron, a clear paradox. Living while dying. Dying while living.

What do driving experts tell us to do when we are navigating our vehicles on ice and lose control? We are told to lightly pump the brakes and steer *into* the skid. But what is the natural tendency when we are suddenly sliding off the road? Turn the steering wheel away and slam on the brakes! But to not incur damage and stay safe, we must do the opposite of what *feels* like a natural reaction.

For a sacrifice to stay a sacrifice, yet still be living, it must stay on the altar. For us to be living sacrifices, we must continually give up our desires for His destiny, hand over our lust to take on His life, and let go of our own heart to take His hand. Live on His altar.

Drop the Nets

One day as Jesus was walking along the shore of the Sea of Galilee, he saw two brothers—Simon, also called Peter, and Andrew—throwing a net into the water, for they fished for a living. Jesus called out to them, "Come, follow me, and I will show you how to fish for people!" And they left their nets at once and followed him. A little farther up the shore he saw two other brothers, James and John, sitting in a boat with their father, Zebedee, repairing their nets. And he called them to come, too. They immediately followed him, leaving the boat and their father behind. (Matthew 4:18–22)

What made these normal guys take such abrupt action? Did Jesus' words somehow hypnotize them? Did He exert some spiritual power over them? No. These were Jewish men who had as young guys gone through the process of being evaluated by the rabbis. From childhood they had been taught the Torah. When they reached the proper age, a rabbi tested them on their ability to handle the Scripture. If they could repeat memorized passages properly, correctly talk about the context of various verses, and pass the difficult test, the rabbi would say, "Come and follow me" into training. If they did not pass, the rabbi would release them to go find a career, most likely the path of their father.

Jesus had already gained a reputation as a great rabbi, and word had gotten around that something was different with this man. So when He walked up and with no test at all said, "Come and follow Me," that was a huge honor and shock to someone who had flunked the original rabbi test. It was a rare second chance.

"Leaving the boat and their father behind" represented both career and family. Their response to Jesus was an immediate yes.

Let me ask you a question: What is it that you need to "leave behind" to fully commit to follow Christ? What are you holding onto? What is holding you back? It does not even have to be a bad or evil thing. There was nothing wrong with being fishermen, nothing wrong with being in business with dad. That was a good, honest living. Jesus did not spring them from jail to start a gang. He just called normal, simple men to launch a revolution that would change history. That is what He is still doing today! He is calling you to that same revolution.

But not everyone Jesus called "dropped their nets."

Guy #1:

As they were walking along, someone said to Jesus, "I will follow you wherever you go." But Jesus replied, "Foxes have dens to live in, and birds have nests, but the Son of Man has no place even to lay his head." (Luke 9:57–58)

Guy #2:

He said to another person, "Come, follow me." The man agreed, but he said, "Lord, first let me return home and bury my father." But Jesus told him, "Let the spiritually dead bury their own dead! Your duty is to go and preach about the Kingdom of God." (Luke 9:59–60)

Guy #3:

Another said, "Yes, Lord, I will follow you, but first let me say good-bye to my family." But Jesus told him, "Anyone who puts a hand to the plow and then looks back is not fit for the Kingdom of God." (Luke 9:61–62)

At first read, Jesus' responses seem harsh. But in every instance, the men were giving cultural excuses. He also knew their hearts and that they were just trying to sound good. They were being politically correct and did not mean what they were saying. Jesus was essentially calling their bluff.

Now as for yourself, only you and God know what you need to do to become a living sacrifice. Only you and God know what you have to drop to find your place with Him. But what Goliath do you need to cut the head off of, so you can walk with Jesus in freedom? Before you can follow Him, your heart has to be ready to go. That was exactly the point of what Jesus said to these three men.

If Jesus appeared to you right now and said, "Let's talk. Tell me what you need Me to do for you," what would you say?

What would you want changed? What would you hand over? What would need to be sacrificed? What nets would you have to drop?

Defeating the Me Monster

In the title of this chapter, I mentioned "the Me Monster." That concept comes from one of my favorite comedians: Brian Regan. His bits on UPS, Little League, family vacations, and a myriad of other everyday topics make me laugh out loud even when I am completely alone. He has one routine called "Dinner Party" you can find on YouTube. In the clip he talks about the Me Monster, the guy in the room who goes on and on talking about himself—what he has done, what he owns, where he has been, and how his life is so much better than anyone else's in the room.

Well, as we know, there is a Me Monster in us all. I am a Me Monster. You are a Me Monster. It is a clever, funny way to describe our flesh. But to follow Jesus, the Me Monster stands in defiance and, well, he has to die on the altar, become a living sacrifice.

Revelation 5 is one of the most powerful, dramatic passages in all of Scripture because the words tell us with such majesty and power who defeated sin. Take this in, because your life is indeed found here.

And I saw a strong angel, who shouted with a loud voice: "Who is worthy to break the seals on this scroll and open it?" But no one in heaven or on earth or under the earth was able to open the scroll and read it.

Then I began to weep bitterly because no one was found worthy to open the scroll and read it. But one of the twenty-four elders said to me, "Stop weeping! Look, the Lion of the tribe of Judah, the heir to David's throne, has won the victory. He is worthy to open the scroll and its seven seals."

Then I saw a Lamb that looked as if it had been slaughtered, but it was now standing between the throne and the four living beings and among the twenty-four elders. He had seven horns and seven eyes, which represent the sevenfold Spirit of God that is sent out into every part of the earth. He stepped forward and took the scroll from the right hand of the one sitting on the throne. And when he took the scroll, the four living beings and the twenty-four elders fell down before the Lamb. Each one had a harp, and they held gold bowls filled with incense, which are the prayers of God's people. And they sang a new song with these words:

"You are worthy to take the scroll and break its seals and open it. For you were slaughtered, and your blood has ransomed people for God from every tribe and language and people and nation. And you have caused them to become a Kingdom of priests for our God. And they will reign on the earth."

Then I looked again, and I heard the voices of thousands and millions of angels around the throne and of the living beings and the elders. And they sang in a mighty chorus: "Worthy is the Lamb who was slaughtered—to receive power and riches and wisdom and strength and honor and glory and blessing." (Revelation 5:2–12)

There is only One who can right our wrongs.

There is only One who can lead and empower us to right the wrongs in our world.

There is only One who can defeat the Me Monster.

His name is Jesus.

Part Four

Believing,

Becoming,

Being

a Man After

God's Heart

Chapter Fifteen

Pagans into Priests, Prodigals into Princes

And the Lord—who is the Spirit—makes us more and more like him as we are changed into his glorious image.
—*2 Corinthians 3:18*

Let's look at how God changes us as men from several vantage points of inspiration—men who can pursue His heart and be empowered to do everything He asks of us by and through His Spirit.

God Changes Pagans into Priests

In the slang, a pagan is someone that has little to no religion and cares mostly about selfish pleasures. A priest has a calling from God to serve Him and people. Scripture is clear that regardless of vocational calling, *every* man who accepts

Christ as Lord turns from pagan to priest. The transition from godless to God-seeking, from religion to relationship, enacts a ministry calling on our lives to be used by Him. That is what *Lord* means. What we do for a paycheck—whether clerk, corporate, construction, or clergy—does not matter, because the purpose of our lives is no longer for ourselves, but to serve Him and bring His will onto the earth. What we do for a living should just finance our ministry. (I encourage you to think on that statement for a moment, if you have never considered the concept.)

You are royal priests, a holy nation, God's very own possession. As a result, you can show others the goodness of God, for he called you out of the darkness into his wonderful light. (1 Peter 2:9)

Jesus turns us from men who do not or will not acknowledge God into men called and ordained into His service. No matter if anyone told you that you were a champion or a chump, first string or third string, A-List or Loser's List, no longer matters. In Christ, you count. You matter. He assigns you as a priest into His kingdom.

A priest has the authority and ability to not only speak to Him directly anytime, but also to intervene on His behalf in people's lives. Christ's work on the cross tore the curtain between God and man so anyone who receives Him can go straight to Jesus for himself, his family, and anyone to whom God calls that man to minister (ref. Matthew 27:50–51; Hebrews 4:15–16).

What does a pagan do? Whatever he wants, because life is meaningless and there is no God. Does anything truly matter if there is nothing past this life? No.

What does a priest do? He does the will and the work of God. What else matters when eternity is at stake? Nothing.

But the rampant, systemic problem we have in Western-culture Christianity is that many who claim to be priests are behaving like pagans. But no matter what you may have done even up to this very day, God wants to use you to be His agent of change in the world. He wants you to hear Him, apply His words, and bring His kingdom to earth right where you are. Redeem the lost. Save the perishing. Rescue the captives. (ref. Isaiah 42)

This most-noble calling is the only way I know to be certain we do not waste our lives. We will not get to the end of the race and look back in regret. We will hit the tape at the finish line of life, ready to face Him. Why? Because we followed Jesus to the end.

All glory to him who loves us and has freed us from our sins by shedding his blood for us. He has made us a Kingdom of priests for God his Father. All glory and power to him forever and ever! Amen. (Revelation 1:5–6)

God Changes Prodigals into Princes

I suppose it is arguable whether I am a true prodigal in the biblical view of the word or I just did not fully understand the Christ-life at age twelve. By the sixth grade, I had never darkened the door of a church in our small Texas town. Some friends invited me to what they called "Sunday school." (Can I just say to a lost kid that does not sound appealing on any level.) But as with most of us, relationships won out because my buddies invited me, so I went to see what school on Sunday looked like.

A dozen young boys who all knew each other well herded into this little room and the teacher began to speak. The sweet, kind, elderly retired man talked about things we do that are wrong. (Okay, you've got me. I'll admit that's true. Keep talking.)

He then said those wrong things called sin make the God who created us very unhappy. (Well, dang. I just found out there's a God and now He's already upset with me. I didn't even know He existed a few minutes ago, and now there's this bad news. Not good, but okay, keep going, sir. I'll hear you out.)

He talked a bit about Hell and being separated from God because of sin. (I had heard of that place before. My dad mentioned it a few times when he got angry. But now it made total sense that people tell you to go there when they're ticked at you.)

Next, the man told us that this same God came down in the form of a man named Jesus and He sacrificed His life for mine, so I could go to Heaven and be with Him and would not have to go to Hell. (Okay, this is *really* good news. I like this plot twist. This makes a lot of sense. So glad to know I have an option other than Hell.)

Let's review from a twelve-year-old boy's perspective: I do bad things that God does not like. Because God is perfect and just, that condemns me to a place of eternal fire. But He made a way to change this outcome through believing that His Son died in my place because He is also loving and merciful. He offers me a room in His home in Heaven. (Sounds like a no-brainer. Wonder what the catch is? Oh well, count me in.)

So I silently prayed the prayer for salvation. But I did not understand this offer included a lifestyle that could be lived *with* this God. I understood salvation to be a one-time event when it was really a lifelong relationship.

Fast forward to nineteen years old. Now I am a musician who just wants to be a rock star. (Back when classic rock was still just current rock.) My prayer for salvation seven years prior is a misunderstood memory. I am far away from God, the church, the Bible, all things Christian. The new music minister at the church called me one day, which was quite weird. He invited me to play drums on a weeklong church choir trip. I had really long, thick, parted-in-the-middle, hippie-style hair and dressed accordingly. I also had a massive drum set, which I had heard a lot of church people believed Satan himself had invented. This music minister knew all about me but called anyway. Needless to say, he had a *lot* of guts.

Much to my own surprise and threat to my personal hip factor, I accepted. (Little did I know at the time, but this was actually God coming after one of his wayward sons.) I really did not understand why I was saying yes. But while the minister gave the invitation, the Holy Spirit was throwing the party. That week I hung out with Christ followers, played at a church every night, and was re-introduced to Scripture, worship, fellowship, and introduced to this new paradigm called discipleship. And the biggest part, I got loved on in spite of myself, how I acted, and how I looked. I was cared for because of just who I was, not what I did. (Man, who does that?)

About four nights in, a light bulb went off in my spirit. The reason that the last seven years had been miserable was because I was on the wrong road. The ladder I had been trying to climb was on the wrong building. You know how when you realize you are lost on a highway and cannot figure out if you should just keep driving or turn around, but you know you have no clue where you are? That was me doing life.

Well, I came home and did a one-eighty. I shut the door on my past and walked into a new life. I hated that I had wasted several years, but I was thankful I was finally shown the right road. I was grateful the same Father who made sure I heard about Him also made sure I was able to make my way back to Him, to find my way home.

Jesus told a story about a young man who got bored with the family farm and told his dad he wanted him to go ahead and give him the inheritance money he would receive upon his father's death. He did not want to wait on daddy's demise. He was going to go live some life now. He cashed the check; said goodbye to his dad, brother, and family; and ventured out for the good life.

The short story is he blew through the money really fast by living high, and ended up feeding pigs to make enough money to eat. Before long, the pig food was starting to look good to him so he decided he would risk going back home rather than die in a mud hole far away. But long before he got to his dad's house, he was shocked at what he saw on the road.

"And while he was still a long way off, his father saw him coming. Filled with love and compassion, he ran to his son, embraced him, and kissed him. His son said to him, 'Father, I have sinned against both heaven and you, and I am no longer worthy of being called your son.' But his father said to the servants, 'Quick! Bring the finest robe in the house and put it on him. Get a ring for his finger and sandals for his feet. And kill the calf we have been fattening. We must celebrate with a feast, for this son of mine was dead and has now returned to life. He was lost, but now he is found.' So the party began." (Luke 15:20–24)

From a pigsty to a party. That is a great picture of God's salvation.

Some of you reading this book have a prodigal-son testimony, whether from many years of rebellion or a brief trek on the wild side in college. Maybe you are a prodigal who has not found his way home yet. Regardless of your past or current state, I want you to consider that all of us men are prodigals in two ways.

First, God created each of us to have fellowship with Him. When He formed us in our mothers' wombs, He had high hopes we would choose to spend our lives with Him. But the sin nature drove us to "leave home" and explore the world. Some come home when they are six years old, some as teens, while others as grown men. Sadly, some never make it back home and die out in the far country. But, regardless, that length of time from creation to new creation is a prodigal season for God as Creator and Father. Waiting and watching, He is always working on our behalf until we come home and will not stop until it is too late.

Second, and I will make this a personal example, on any given day I awake as a born-again Christ follower, but within a few hours, sometimes only minutes, I make a choice to "leave home" and take my own path. My motive, attitude, and action causes me to turn my back on my Father God, which takes me to a foreign land, away from His presence, by my own choice.

Whether that decision lasts for minutes, hours, days, or even weeks, living in that state of sin, at any point I can then be convicted, repent, and "return home." He then receives me with open arms. The prodigal process is constantly occurring in our hearts, even when sometimes the only ones who know are the Father and us. In this state, we have not lost our salvation, but we are walking out of fellowship with Him.

Throughout our lives, God constantly desires that this prodigal time become shorter and shorter. The cross always allows for us to come back home, anytime, even many times a day.

Whether you agree with me in this thought does not really matter, because here is the real point: The focus of this passage is not so much about the son's disobedience, but the father's response. Jesus did not tell this particular story to prove how detrimental sin is. He told the story to display the depth of His Father's love. The same love that always brings us back from sin into His presence, from the pigsty to the party.

No matter how long we are gone, how far we fall, how deep we dive, or how depraved the disobedience, He is there. He has already made provision for the redemption of our souls. He has already taken back the keys to death and Hell. He has paid for every debt that we could possibly ever owe in our bankrupt hearts.

So what does God do when we come home? As in Jesus' parable, He restores us not to servanthood but full sonship. He wraps us with His robe of righteousness. He puts the ring with His seal on our finger, allowing us to be involved in His work, accomplishing His purposes by His name (ref. 2 Corinthians 5:21; Ephesians 4:24).

If one of my sons goes the wrong way, is he still my son, bearing my name? Yes, of course. His decision may create consequences, but it does not change his name, who his father is, or who he is.

God's love is not about what we believe we deserve or do not deserve, but about what He wants for our lives. Not about what we have done or not done, but about what He has accomplished on our behalf. He offers each of us as men, every moment of every day, the opportunity to no longer be prodigals in search of significance and satisfaction, but to be princes—sons of the King—acting under His authority, residing in His kingdom.

We become His sons who choose to only serve the Father. But first, we have to head down the road toward Home, toward the Father. Repent. Change our minds. Do an about-face. Turn around.

Take in the offer God makes and the promises He gives:

> *"Hey there! All who are thirsty, come to the water!*
> *Are you penniless? Come anyway—buy and eat!*

Come, buy your drinks, buy wine and milk.
Buy without money—everything's free!
Why do you spend your money on junk food,
your hard-earned cash on cotton candy?
Listen to me, listen well: Eat only the best,
fill yourself with only the finest.
Pay attention, come close now,
listen carefully to my life-giving, life-nourishing words.
I'm making a lasting covenant commitment with you,
the same that I made with David: sure, solid, enduring love.
I set him up as a witness to the nations,
made him a prince and leader of the nations,
And now I'm doing it to you:
You'll summon nations you've never heard of,
and nations who've never heard of you
will come running to you
Because of me, your GOD,
because The Holy of Israel has honored you."
Seek GOD while he's here to be found,
pray to him while he's close at hand.
Let the wicked abandon their way of life
and the evil their way of thinking.
Let them come back to GOD, who is merciful,
come back to our God, who is lavish with forgiveness.
(Isaiah 55:1–7 MSG)

Chapter Sixteen

Lepers into Leaders, Traitors into Translators, Fugitives into Friends

"Who needs a doctor: the healthy or the sick?
I'm here inviting outsiders, not insiders—
an invitation to a changed life,
changed inside and out."
—*Luke 5:31–32* MSG

God Changes Lepers into Leaders

I do not know about you, but I have never had a devastating skin disease where you lose feeling in your extremities and then ultimately your limbs. I have never felt the shame and rejection from people who would not come near me, touch me, or even look at me.

Leprosy was a common but serious and contagious health threat in the days of Jesus. The disease created a society of people who were shunned by the masses, left to devastating isolation and loneliness, desperately in need of love and healing. For that very reason, Jesus spent a good amount of time with them (ref. Luke 7:21–22).

Bottom line is no one *chose* to be around a leper except Jesus. When everyone was running from them, He was walking toward them.

Leaders are people who go before the crowd to blaze trails, forge new paths, and discover uncharted territory. If we call someone a leader, we are also saying that people are following. A friend once told me, "If you think you're a leader, but look behind you and no one is following, then guess what? You're not a leader. But if you don't believe you're a leader, yet you look behind you and people are following, then guess what? You're a leader!" So ultimately, it is not so much about the perception of the person leading as it is about the followers.

Social media has somewhat altered the definition and connotation of a leader because a celebrity can have a million followers but not be a leader on any level. In fact, they could be holed up in their mansion with a small entourage who are all on the payroll. Ironic how social media is not about leadership, just all about following.

Christ can take men from shunned, rejected, and unloved spiritual, social, and emotional lepers into leaders. Men others will want to follow who before no one would have given a second thought. I have seen this process occur many times over my forty years of ministry. Nothing changes a man and converts him to a leader like Jesus. I have also watched God give men countless resources and opportunities to change and lead but see them refuse Him and His offer. Staying status quo and comfortable is often just too tempting, and is one of the biggest traps a man can face.

One of the most incredible sights is seeing God get hold of a modern-day leper. He begins to talk to and listen to the Lord. He begins to read and apply Scripture. He begins to enter into accountable relationships for the purpose of protection and growth. He begins to heed the wisdom of a multitude of counselors. He begins to pay attention to his family. He begins to emerge out of his long-isolated life. People start to matter. You see the "leper" start to get his feeling back. Healing comes. A leader emerges out of a once desperate, hopeless situation.

When we live in isolation from years of spiritual and emotional numbness brought on by personal failure and shame, doesn't that produce a similar outcome as leprosy in this culture? I have certainly felt the personal effects of this version of the disease myself.

Here is the story of when Jesus turned a real leper into a leader.

As Jesus continued on toward Jerusalem, he reached the border between Galilee and Samaria. As he entered a village there, ten men with leprosy stood at a distance, crying out, "Jesus, Master, have mercy on us!"

He looked at them and said, "Go show yourselves to the priests." And as they went, they were cleansed of their leprosy.

One of them, when he saw that he was healed, came back to Jesus, shouting, "Praise God!" He fell to the ground at Jesus' feet, thanking him for what he had done. This man was a Samaritan.

Jesus asked, "Didn't I heal ten men? Where are the other nine? Has no one returned to give glory to God except this foreigner?" And Jesus said to the man, "Stand up and go. Your faith has healed you." (Luke 17:11–19)

So how do I know this one healed leper became a leader? Because the moment he realized he was healed, he stopped following, going along with the crowd, and went alone to worship the Lord.

That is a sure sign of a leader changed by God.

God Changes Traitors into Translators

One of my favorite TV characters of all time was Jack Bauer on the show *24*. Just like so many folks, I watched one episode somewhere around the second season and I was hooked. A major reason I was drawn to the special government agent that Kiefer Sutherland portrayed is because Jack could put all personal feelings aside and do the right thing in every circumstance, regardless of who agreed with him and even if no one else would help.

Jack would go against the grain in a heartbeat to ensure justice and patriotism prevailed. Over one hundred and ninety-two episodes, thousands upon thousands of men found a hero in Jack Bauer. Why? You could count on Jack. Jack would get it done, no matter how impossible the odds. Jack would undergo any personal sacrifice to get to the truth.

Another great aspect of *24* plots was there was always a clear line drawn between the good guys and the bad guys, a clear distinction between agents and terrorists. But there was always a third group you could count on too, even though it took a while to figure out who they were: traitors.

They appeared to be good guys, but were really just bad guys in disguise. Of course, eventually the truth always came to light and Jack would go after the bad guys *and* the traitors. He never liked bad guys, but he always held a special place in his heart for traitors. To Jack, at least the bad guys had the guts to be bad guys out in the open. Traitors were just above worm scum to him, and he eventually let them know his deepest feelings in a showdown. Jack always personally dealt with the traitors.

But that was just a TV show. What does God do with traitors? After all, contrary to the popular belief of many, He is not an American citizen. First, here are some words we associate with a traitor: turncoat, defector, deserter, anyone who betrays their original loyalties. And yes, a Judas.

While I've got good news for you, first, some bad news. I am a traitor. Yeah. I sit and eat with Jesus, but then hours later kiss Him on the cheek and turn away to cooperate with the Enemy in some thought I have, some attitude I cop, some words I speak, some action I take. Isn't that the reality of choosing to sin as a Christ follower? Repeating the Judas experience over and over?

How many times have I declared my allegiance to Christ with my hand held in the air in praise, my eyes filled with tears of gratitude, my lips declaring His goodness, and my heart filled with love, only to find within hours, I am selling Him out, turning my back, choosing my way, and acting as if I do not know Him? Can you relate to that at all? Or is it just me who suffers from this seesaw effect? Honestly, this deeply frustrates me about myself. Yeah, by definition of *traitor*, I often betray my God. But again, what does God do with traitors? What does He do with me, with you, when we trade our loyalty?

Let's go back to Jack Bauer for a moment. What if he captured the traitor and he/she turned out to be a hostile foreign agent? Jack looked the person in the eyes and in his menacing voice gritted out, "Look, I'm not going to kill you. I'm not going to hurt you. I'm going to spare your life so you can help me translate the message of the hope and freedom in America to your fellow countrymen." (Wait. . . . What? . . . No!)

God takes that very strange and paradoxical approach with traitors.

He takes a man whom He knows can betray Him at the very next turn and tells Him to be a translator in his culture, in His name. Why would God do such a thing? Isn't there a better plan? Evidently not. Because God knows if a traitor keeps receiving forgiveness and understanding that, over time, the joy of watching Him change lives through the translation of his life will overcome the desire to betray. Yes, the sanctification process is often very slow for some of us, but it works.

Whether we have followed Christ for three months or thirty years, one of the very things that makes us love Him more as time passes is His great grace and continued desire to use us in His work, in spite of ourselves. The fact that He wants to involve us in the miracle of helping Him change lives begins to slowly overcome our desire to betray Him in our sin. We begin to see that translating the love of God to our culture is far more satisfying and gratifying than trying to do life on our own, away from Him.

Meanwhile, Saul was uttering threats with every breath and was eager to kill the Lord's followers. So he went to the high priest. He requested letters addressed to the synagogues in Damascus, asking for their cooperation in the arrest of any followers of the Way he found there. He wanted to bring them—both men and women—back to Jerusalem in chains. (Acts 9:1–2)

Saul was a traitor who became Paul, a translator.

This means that anyone who belongs to Christ has become a new person. The old life is gone; a new life has begun! And all of this is a gift from God, who brought us back to himself through Christ. And God has given us this task of reconciling people to him. For God was in Christ, reconciling the world to himself, no longer counting people's sins against them. And he gave us this wonderful message of reconciliation. So we are Christ's ambassadors; God is making his appeal through us. We speak for Christ when we plead, "Come back to God!" (2 Corinthians 5:17–20)

Paul went from an enemy being written about to an ally doing the writing. Translating a heavenly language understandable on earth. God wants you to join Him in this same task, reaching the world for Him, with Him, by Him. What greater purpose could your life serve than following Him and watching Him translate His love through you to others? Changing the world one heart at a time. Turning other traitors into translators. Just like me. Just like you.

God Changes Fugitives into Friends

Ever since the Garden of Eden episode, the world has been full of fugitives. What did Adam and Eve do after they sinned? They ran away and hid from God. Just like a fugitive. Commit the crime. Realize guilt. Try to avoid consequences. Run!

Do you remember playing with your buddies in the neighborhood or at school and someone would get hurt, break something, or do something stupid? What do all little boys do? Run! Scatter! There is even a phrase you yell out when a dirty deed occurs: "Every man for himself!" Why? Because when something bad happened, you did not want to just stand there and take the blame; you ran and hid.

Running away from responsibility and consequence is a *natural* response. You may have just been standing there daydreaming, picking your nose, but when you realized everyone else ran, so did you. Don't wait around to find out why, just take off.

But as we get older, we get cooler about our sin, don't we? . . . Or do we? We tend to make sure the things we do that we do not feel so good about, happen at night or at least in the dark. Nightclubs are not called nightclubs for no reason. Prostitutes do not fill the street corners at 8:00 a.m. Men do not have their mistresses meet them out in front of their house and leave her car parked in the driveway. Most thieves wait until nightfall sets in to break in. Why? We just *naturally* know to do our bad things in the dark, away from the light, out of plain sight.

As the Scriptures say, "No one is righteous—not even one. No one is truly wise; no one is seeking God. All have turned away; all have become useless. No one does good, not a single one." (Romans 3:10–12)

We are all fugitives.

In the classic movie *The Fugitive* with Harrison Ford and Tommy Lee Jones, the climactic scene occurs when Dr. Richard Kimble (Ford) is trying to escape—again—from Chief Deputy Marshal Gerard (Jones) down in the laundry room of the hotel after he has confronted Dr. Nichols, who we now know is behind the murder and cover-up.

Gerard calls out, "Kimble! I know you didn't kill your wife!" Everyone lets out a huge sigh of relief at that moment. And most especially Dr. Kimble. Why? Because we all knew that finally almost two hours of running and narrow escapes could stop. At last, there could be relief from running. No more hiding.

How many of us have a good life, but we can't seem to stop running and hiding. Running from our past. Hiding from failure. Running from responsibility. Hiding from facing our own hearts. And too often, running and hiding from whom we know God has called us to be.

But why do we run? Even if no one can actually tell we are running. What are we afraid will happen if we stop? Do we not think that God can catch us if He wants? Here is a verse to help us put things in perspective.

I no longer call you slaves, because a master doesn't confide in his slaves. Now you are my friends, since I have told you everything the Father told me. (John 15:15)

You cannot make friends with someone you are running away from, can you? The sooner we figure out that Jesus is standing in the same place where He has always been, then we know exactly where to go to meet our Friend.

God wants the death and resurrection of His Son to stop the running, to end the hiding, for us to accept that He has paid our ransom and offered us redemption and freedom. Today, He desires to be *your* Friend. Today, you can be *His* friend.

Fugitives might be seeking the truth like Dr. Kimble, but their first objective is to keep running and hiding. But real friends do not run away; they seek you out, just like Jesus.

The Three S's

We can be changed from a pagan to a priest, a prodigal to a prince, a leper to a leader, a traitor to a translator, and a fugitive to a friend when we agree to:

Surrender ➡ Submit ➡ Serve

Surrender means to give up the fight, give over control, abandon your rights, and declare defeat.

Submit means to yield to, agree to, or defer to.

Serve means to put another's needs before your own.

The biblical process of surrender and submission is giving up our lives and taking on Christ's. After this process has begun, the assignment is to serve. But here is the cool thing that took me a very long time to understand—and I am still working on it daily: God does not bark out orders, telling us to get out of His face and get to work. He walks with us as a Friend, and we work together as a team. He does this with all His followers.

As you navigate to continue to allow God to change you, remember the three S's—Surrender, Submit, and Serve, in that order. When you mess up and disobey God, simply ask His forgiveness. No wallowing. No emotional beat-downs. No wasting precious time.

Get right back to the 3 S's ASAP. Surrender, submit, and serve.

Believe, become, be.

Chapter Seventeen

Brothers in the Battle I

Two are better than one,
because they have a good return for their labor:
If either of them falls down,
one can help the other up.
But pity anyone who falls and
has no one to help them up.
. . . Though one may be overpowered,
two can defend themselves.
A cord of three strands is not quickly broken.
—*Ecclesiastes 4:9–10, 12* NIV

I discovered this passage many years ago, and the words as well as the concept immediately struck me as an incredible men's ministry message. So I adopted these verses by calling men's small groups 3SG or Three Strand Groups, using this passage as the foundation. Over the years, outside of having a godly wife, there is nothing I have seen change men into the image of Jesus faster and more efficiently than brothers regularly getting together. Now just meeting for meeting's sake can produce nothing. It is what you do when you gather that makes this paradigm work and change us.

I want to talk about five factors that can create connection and growth that ultimately create a sixth and final factor. First, to help us understand what we do when we meet together, I want to offer a simple analogy. We need two things to fight for and defend one another: a sword and a shield.

From biblical to medieval times, the sword was primarily an offensive weapon with the shield used for defense. In the dominant hand of the warrior, the sword was wielded to advance while in the lesser hand, the shield defended against attacks. Both were equal and necessary to survive in battle and achieve victory.

As modern metaphors for the Christian man in today's world, the sword represents spiritual growth—transformation into the image of Christ—and the shield, moral protection—proactive efforts to stop the Enemy's attacks. As examples, the commitment to daily prayer is a sword, while accountability with other men to strengthen areas of weakness is a shield.

So when you and your friends meet together, you only focus on two things:

Sword—Offense = Spiritual Growth

Shield—Defense = Moral Protection

If conversations drift to anything other than falling into one of these two categories, you are off track. Next, let's move into the commitments we are making as a group.

Commitment to Environment

We all know that who we hang out with, who we listen to, and whose words fill our minds and hearts make a major difference in who we are becoming in any season of life. For the Christ follower, environment is always crucial.

Most people do not get through childhood without experiencing the joy and tragedy of owning a goldfish. Joy because they are fun to watch swim around and explore but tragedy because they quite often die way too soon. But God placed an interesting survival characteristic in goldfish that makes them unique.

This species of fish will grow to the size their environment can sustain and then they will stop. But if later they are introduced into a larger setting, the goldfish will start to grow again until once again reaching its instinctive maximum size. People who upgrade their aquariums have reported that their original goldfish will increase in size every time the environment is made larger.

Most of the deer species in the United States have this same characteristic as well. That is why when you see construction and civilization encroaching on a forested area, people also begin to notice the physical size of the deer in the area become smaller.

As Christ followers, we are just like the goldfish and the deer in our spiritual state. We will only grow to the size that our environment allows and then we will stop or stagnate. But if a new catalyst such as a discipleship opportunity or some other inspiration or challenge to grow is introduced, we will begin to mature again. This places the responsibility to stay in a nurturing spiritual environment squarely on our own shoulders.

The challenge of continual growth and maturity was present throughout all of Paul's letters.

And now, just as you accepted Christ Jesus as your Lord, you must continue to follow him. Let your roots grow down into him, and let your lives be built on him. Then your faith will grow strong in the truth you were taught, and you will overflow with thankfulness. (Colossians 2:6–7)

The book of Proverbs has many challenges to our environment.

Become wise by walking with the wise; hang out with fools and watch your life fall to pieces. (Proverbs 13:20 MSG)

The wisdom of the wise keeps life on track; the foolishness of fools lands them in the ditch. (Proverbs 14:8 MSG)

There are two potential character killers regularly found in our environment:

- Intake

What we allow to go into our minds, eyes, ears, and hearts is critical to our growth and defense. For example, the wrong guys around us can bring about very bad intake, while the right men can influence us to grow.

- Isolation

Like the Ecclesiastes passage clearly states, the man alone can get into trouble quickly. My personal opinion is that the majority of American males are the most isolated of any time in history, especially emotionally and spiritually.

God wants to protect our *intake* and end our *isolation* so we can be an *influence* in our culture for Him.

Commitment to Prayer

You may be thinking, *Okay, this is very Christianity 101. I already get the need to pray and how to pray.* Yes, I am sure you do, but for most men, the first things to be punted in a busy life are prayer and Bible reading. We believe they are important, but we do not regularly practice the belief.

Let's define prayer as intentional time to speak with, listen to, and rest in the presence of Christ. Most of us get the first one—*speak*—but miss the next two—*listen* and *rest*. These two disciplines require stillness, quieting the mind, avoiding distractions, inviting the Holy Spirit to speak, and then allowing the time to listen for God's voice.

Before daybreak the next morning, Jesus got up and went out to an isolated place to pray. (Mark 1:35)

Let's take this verse apart in segments to dig into the meaning:

- He got up early.

- He went off by Himself.

- He prayed.

You don't have to study the Greek language, because the verse means exactly what it says in any translation or paraphrase you read. Jesus got up early in the morning and went away alone to pray for a single, simple purpose—to spend one-on-one time with His Father. We clearly see here from His example that a dedicated daily time alone with God is one of the most life-changing spiritual disciplines we can invest in. No distractions, devices, or noise, and no one else around—just you and God.

When it comes to money, the amounts we all make vary widely. Many factors that would distinguish us from one another would be a massive range of difference. But that is not true with time. There are seven days in everyone's week, with twenty-four hours in each day. That is one hundred sixty-eight hours (168) every week.

Imagine going to your local big-box hardware store and heading to the department that sells chains. Whether you choose the iron or plastic variety, think about rolling out 168 links on the concrete floor and cutting it off after the final link. If each link is two inches long, the total chain would be twenty-eight feet.

Now with your chain stretched out in a line to represent the hours in your week, let's say you pray fifteen minutes every day, which would be a major commitment for a lot of guys.

In your chain, that would be almost 2 of your 168 links (.25 or 15 minutes a day X 7 days a week). Interesting perspective, huh? When we look at time represented by a physical line with each link of the chain being an hour, fifteen minutes a day seems very manageable. You may decide to go for thirty minutes a day, or almost 4 links of the 168.

The bottom line of this visual analogy representing a commitment to daily prayer is not to invoke guilt. That is always useless and discouraging. The challenge is to see prayer as a major investment of 2 or 4 hours a week into the other 166 or 164 hours!

If prayer is a new discipline for you or you realize you only tend to pray when there's a crisis, then the great news is you can start fresh today. Allow me to make a recommendation: Let's say you are going to commit to ten minutes a day for the next seven days. Spend the first six minutes telling God anything you want Him to know. Then spend a minute in total stillness, deep breathing, and quieting your heart. Next pray, "Speak, Lord, I'm listening. Tell me what You want me to know." Then for your final three minutes, just listen for Him to speak to your heart.

For more help on establishing a prayer time or just deepening in your prayers, here are a few practical details spelled out:

While spending a few moments alone with God first thing in the morning can be best to set the pace for your day, choose when will be optimum for your schedule. You may need to experiment a bit, but pick a time and stick with it. We will all make time for the things that matter most to us.

Just like Jesus in Mark 1:35, you need a quiet and peaceful setting. Pick the most comfortable place you can find, away from distractions. No phones. No devices. No TV and no one else around. Your environment is crucial for you to be focused as you engage with God.

Allow time each day to speak with God and tell Him everything as you would a best friend. Just talk to Him. Tell Him your heart. Be honest. Be specific. No fancy spiritual language is necessary. Learning to pray or deepening in your prayers could revolutionize your life and spiritual growth. Be mindful to keep praying as you go through your day, and maintain an ongoing dialogue with your heavenly Father. Remember, He does not stay in your prayer spot but goes with you everywhere.

Close your time with a quiet moment to hear God speak. Be still and know He is God (Psalm 46:10). Quiet your mind and heart and pray the prayer of Samuel: *"Speak, LORD, for your servant is listening" (1 Samuel 3:9).* It is normal to feel a little strange at first as you sit and listen, but if you stick with this discipline, you will be amazed at what the Holy Spirit will speak to you. Then obey what you hear and live out what He tells you. The goal of this time is to allow Jesus to change your life through a personal relationship with Him.

Commitment to Scripture

We are living in a post-Christian society as well as a Westernized church culture that as a whole no longer values the Word of God. Actually teaching the Scripture and its practical application for life is unfortunately too much of a rarity among churches today.

If you have never made a commitment to regularly reading the Bible or for some reason reading Scripture has become stale and you have abandoned the discipline, please prayerfully and carefully take in this section to re-engage. In regard to God's words, Moses told the people, *"They are not just idle words for you—they are your life" (Deuteronomy 32:47 NIV).* The same is true for us today.

Let's say it is your birthday and a friend gives you an envelope. You open it to find a gift card inside. The friend did not write how much money is on the card, so you know you will have to go online to find the balance. Because of the relationship, you believe the card has some value, but you have no idea how much until you can check later.

The popularity of giving gift cards is because they are readily available in retail stores and online. They are quick and easy to get and require no attention or imagination to give. Gift cards are not specifically for anyone, can even be given away for someone else to use, and are generic in nature.

When any of us open our Bibles, we can randomly read through passages out of duty or guilt, because "Christians are supposed to read God's Word." This approach to Scripture is a lot like receiving a gift card. We know it has some value but do not really feel it is personal to our lives. The Bible is available everywhere, and anyone can read it anytime (at least in the Western Hemisphere).

Now back to the birthday analogy. What if a family member hands you a card and inside is a personal check made out to you for $500? You immediately know by looking at it exactly who gave it to you, that it is specifically for you, and exactly the value it has. It is not generic for anyone, but is specific to you. The gift is personal and the value expressed from the giver to you is immediate.

As Christ followers, engaging with our Bibles should be like receiving a personal check. When we find His message for us in His Word, we know through the power of the Holy Spirit speaking to us that God gave it. We know by faith the message is for us, and we know exactly the value it has in our lives. The gift is personal and the value expressed from the Giver is immediate.

What is the real difference in this gift-card and personal-check example? Two things: Expectation and attitude. We tend to get out what we put into Scripture and our attitude toward reading impacts what we receive from the pages.

The gift card represents religion. The personal check represents a relationship.

Every day, God writes a "personal check" to each of us in the form of a message from His Word. His eternal truth comes to meet our needs and desires for the day, and inside He speaks intimate words to provide an invaluable gift for us.

Another analogy, which is not original to me, is receiving junk mail versus a love letter. One is scanned and tossed, because it means little or nothing. The other is targeted for the heart and is personal. One is barely read, while the other is scoped over and over in detail.

So do you want to read junk mail or a love letter? Do you want a gift card or a personal check? God has already promised which one He will deliver today. The choice of what you receive from Him is up to you.

For the word of God is alive and powerful. It is sharper than the sharpest two-edged sword, cutting between soul and spirit, between joint and marrow. It exposes our innermost thoughts and desires. (Hebrews 4:12)

In addition to all of these, hold up the shield of faith to stop the fiery arrows of the devil. Put on salvation as your helmet, and take the sword of the Spirit, which is the word of God. (Ephesians 6:16–17)

Where I'm from in Texas, seeing cows standing around in a pasture constantly chewing is a common sight. Cattle are ruminating animals, meaning they can store food in their stomach called "cud," which is a mixture of digested grass and water. Then whenever the cow wants sustenance, the cud is simply called up to the animal's mouth and it begins chewing. When finished, the cow swallows the cud again. Cattle are constantly repeating this process of rumination, which is a critical part of their health and diet.

I have a good friend in Texas who for thirty-plus years has been an expert animal scientist. His clients bring him in to examine and make recommendations for their herds to keep the cattle healthy and the business profitable. The first thing he does when he arrives at a herd is to see how many of them are ruminating—chewing their cud. He says that in a healthy herd, one-third up to one-half should be ruminating at any given time. If the first thing he notices is a strong-enough percentage *not* ruminating, something is wrong or the herd is sick. He then stops figuring out how to maximize the herd and begins steps to fix the issue and get them healthy again.

The rumination process in cattle has an interesting connection to our consumption of God's Word.

"Blessed is the one who does not walk in step with the wicked or stand in the way that sinners take or sit in the company of mockers, but whose delight is in the law of the Lord, and who meditates on his law, day and night. That person is like a tree planted by streams of water, which yields its fruit in season and whose leaf does not wither—whatever they do prospers." (Psalm 1:1–3 NIV)

When we get to the phrase—*"who meditates on his law, day and night"*—one question men often ask is, "So are we really supposed to read and meditate on God's Word twenty-four-seven? How could we possibly even do that?"

The word ruminate also means "to go over in the mind repeatedly and often casually or slowly" and "to engage in contemplation and reflect."[7] This is where we get the saying, "Let me chew on that awhile before I make a decision." Just as a cow can ruminate at any time on its food, we can *ruminate* on our "food for thought." But this concept goes to a deeper place for the Christ follower.

Meditating on God's Word offers a "cow cud" affect in us. Essentially, when we regularly take in the Word of God, it goes down into our spiritual gut—the soul—and provides sustenance, much like the grass and water combo does for the cow. Then, when we are in any situation where the Word is needed—such as what to do when we are tempted, aren't sure what to say to a friend, we don't know how to answer a difficult question, or respond in a crisis—our spirits "burp up the cud"—the Word into our minds—and we speak it into the situation. Afterwards, we then swallow it back down for another time. The beautiful aspect of this process is *every* Scripture that goes into our spirits can be used by *the* Spirit to minister when needed.

Anytime you are silently praying for wisdom or don't have a clue what to say and a Scripture "just randomly pops into your mind" and you speak or act on it—that is the Psalm 1 rumination principle at work.

Look at how The Message Bible expresses Psalm 1:2: *"Instead you thrill to God's Word, you chew on Scripture day and night."* Meditating is letting our minds "chew on" the passage until we understand what it means for our own lives. You do more than simply read or memorize the verse; instead, you let its meaning become personal, changing who you are and the way you think to be like Christ.

We all know that shelter, water, and food are basic human needs. For the Christ follower, our basic spiritual needs are a growing environment (shelter), prayer (water), and the Word (food). Just as we have to maintain our physical needs to survive in the world, so must we maintain our spiritual needs to thrive as God leads us in our lives.

Chapter Eighteen

Brothers in the Battle II

Friends come and friends go,
but a true friend sticks by you like family.
—Proverbs 18:24 MSG

In this final chapter, let's discuss the second half of the six commitments.

Commitment to Accountability

I mentioned accountability in a previous chapter, but here we will take a deeper dive.

Accountability is everywhere in our lives—laws, speed limits, tests, evaluations, job performance reviews, etc.—to create discipline and protection for society.

The Calgary Stampede in Canada is known as one of the premier rodeos in the world. One of their most exciting events is the Heavy Horse Pull. Teams of two large plow horses are harnessed to a sled on which weights are placed, to see which team can pull the most.

The reason for the tandem pull is this: Alone, a first-place horse can pull 9,000 pounds while a second-place horse can pull 8,000 pounds. But when teamed up in a tandem harness, they can pull how much? Well, 9,000 + 8,000 is 17,000, right? No. Together, these two horses can pull up to 30,000 pounds! How? The principle is called synergy—separate agents working together have a greater total effect than the sum of their individual efforts. Much more can be done in a team effort than can be accomplished solo. Like the plow horses, no matter our individual strength, we are far stronger together.

Accountability creates synergy as we work together in a team of men, whether three or three hundred. We have previously used Ecclesiastes 4:9–12, but it bears repeating again in this context.

Two are better than one, because they have a good return for their labor: If either of them falls down, one can help the other up. But pity anyone who falls and has no one to help them up. . . . Though one may be overpowered, two can defend themselves. A cord of three strands is not quickly broken. (v. 9–10, 12 NIV)

Years ago, a large men's ministry movement swept the country and a lot of guys started accountability groups after those meetings. As I have traveled the country speaking the past ten years, I have met a lot of men who were once in some of those groups. But you would have difficulty finding a group that still meets today. Why? Just because the ministry folded? No, of course not. That had no real bearing on those men's decisions to continue meeting. After talking to many of them, my personal opinion is there is not a clear understanding between disclosure and accountability.

Disclosure is simply sharing and confessing life details to one another. This is much like a parishioner would speak to a priest. The priest can speak forgiveness and a prayer but takes no personal action. Accountability is giving another man permission to help you start an action or stop an action. This means being so intentional that you invite a man to get into your business. Here are some examples:

Disclosure: "I'm struggling with porn."

Accountability: "I'm going to install a program that will email you if I go to a site I shouldn't. Then I want you to contact me if you receive one."

Disclosure: "Every time I go on a business trip to a major city, I end up finding somewhere to gamble."

Accountability: "I'm going on a business trip this next week. I'm asking you to call me at ten p.m. each night and ask me if I'm in my hotel room to stay. Then if I'm not or I plan on leaving, I'll have to lie to you, which I don't want to do."

Disclosure: "Almost every night after I get home from work, I end up drinking way too much."

Accountability: "I'm on my way to your house with all my whiskey. Would you go with me to an AA meeting? I want to be sure I follow through this time."

We could go on and on with all kinds of examples. Disclosure is constantly expressing the problem. Accountability is coming up with solutions to get real help with the problem. Disclosure is a Chihuahua and accountability is a Doberman. One just barks a lot and the other actually guards and protects. Sure, lying and deceit will always be an option, but disclosure makes that way too easy. At least accountability offers some fail-safes along the way.

Confession and prayer are vitally important aspects of guys helping one another to grow and mature. But that's where real helps *begins*. There are going to be situations in all our lives that need some extra steps to provide answers to on-going struggles. That is why accountability should be a weapon in our arsenal.

We cannot just use one another as personal priests to confess, but we also have to create intimacy with each other as brothers in Christ to convert our behavior into Christ-likeness. To believe, become, be.

Accountability helps eliminate secrets, running and hiding. The ultimate goal is for our private life to mirror our public life. We are the same men alone as we are with our families, at work, or in a crowded room.

Commitment to Principles

Just like accountability, I mentioned principles in a previous chapter, but here we will also dig deeper into this helpful discipline.

A principle is a self-imposed, predetermined guideline, based on God's Word, you abide by on a short-term or long-term basis. A principle is making a decision once and then simply living by it.

Setting a principle is making a decision about what your actions or reactions will be *before* you are in the situation. Waiting to make a decision until you face a temptation often leads to a wrong choice. A principle can help you avoid this completely.

Just like daily showering and shaving is a habit you do not even think about—you just do it—protecting yourself morally and working to grow spiritually should become a habit and discipline as well.

Satan hates principles because he wants us to have to decide again and again. He wants us to have to make the decision each time we're faced with a temptation with the goal of wearing us down.

There are offensive principles such as committing to spend daily time with God in prayer or Bible study. There are defensive principles such as deciding to stay away from a certain person or situation. As your small group meets and each of you begins to defeat sin and grow in maturity, you can develop group as well as personal principles to keep you on track as men of integrity and honor. Developing principles with your wife for the health of your marriage can be a great asset in the relationship. Making decisions together on things you need to do or not do can create both freedom and protection for you both.

Commitment to Relationships

As a Christ follower, in all our relationships we are to be a part of discipling and encouraging other believers, while being a witness and encouragement to any non-believers. This is honestly a straightforward and simple biblical worldview. If you know someone knows Jesus, then "be Jesus" by spurring them on to grow and mature. If you know a non-believer, "be Jesus" by living out your faith in a way to attract them to Him.

Let us help each other to love others and to do good. (Hebrews 10:24 NLV)

Let's recap. As a man who follows Christ, commit to be intentional about:

- Your environment, both to grow and protect yourself

- Spending regular time with God in prayer

- Taking in and making God's Word a daily staple in your spiritual diet

- Creating accountability in your life to grow and protect yourself

- Developing and committing to spiritual principles of growth and protection

- View every relationship in your circles of influence as Jesus would

In the same way, let your light shine before others, that they may see your good deeds and glorify your Father in heaven. (Matthew 5:16 NIV)

In the Holy Land, the Sea of Galilee is full of life and has beautiful shores. Just a few miles south, the same water flows into the Dead Sea. There is no life there. Everything is dead, hence the name. The reason is it has no outlet, only an inlet. As Christ followers, we must have *both* in our lives.

If you live by these six commitments, you *will* be different. Your life will not reflect religion, but a relationship with Jesus. Matthew 28—the Great Commission—says "as you go" is the best way to share Christ. Even in this culture, no one can debate or argue away a changed life. Living a life of godliness and holiness through the power of the Holy Spirit will make us better men, husbands, fathers, sons, friends, workers, church members, and any role God gives us.

God does not call us to move into the mountains to become religious monks and devote every waking thought only to Him. He does, however, call each of us into a relationship with Him to go into the world, making disciples as we live our lives for Him.

Surveying the Battlefield

Say you and I were placed in a situation where our families were threatened—their safety and their very lives put on the line. We cannot call 9-1-1. We cannot call the police, the Armed Forces, or any outside help. Our only chance is for you and me to rally together to fight the enemy coming to destroy our families and our homes. I don't know about you, but I would want some weapons. In fact, I would prefer an arsenal to call upon. I suppose with enough anger and adrenaline, bare hands might cause some damage, but to hold out and take the enemy completely out, we are going to need some real leverage and support.

Well, gentlemen, in this life, in this world, that really is where we are. There is a definite spiritual battle going on to end our marriages, destroy our children, and take us out. We have an enemy who wants to rob, kill, and destroy (John 10:10), and he'll take any or all of those three he can pull off. Take everything away from you and then go in for the kill. Pick us off one by one. Stop our effectiveness and hurt God.

Here's the truth. Whether you are a Christian or not, a spiritual man or not, you are affected by this battle. You are in it—like it or not, believe it or not. Denying it does not make it untrue. You are either fighting, being fought, or just a pawn in the Enemy's hands.

The war between God and Satan, the angels and demons, the heavenly army and darkness, is happening right now. Just look around you. How far do you have to go in your world to find a family that's crumbling? When was the last time you got bad news about a friend's downfall? Read or watched the news lately? See how everything is going, where we are headed? The battle is real and you know it.

I hope you decide to be certain you are on God's side. To accept His offer to adopt you as His son. To join His army as a warrior for Him. To battle the Enemy. To give your full allegiance to the King of Kings and Lord of Lords.

Final Charge

No, Christian brothers, I do not have that life yet. But I do one thing. I forget everything that is behind me and look forward to that which is ahead of me. My eyes are on the crown. I want to win the race and get the crown of God's call from heaven through Christ Jesus. All of us who are full-grown Christians should think this way. If you do not think this way, God will show it to you. (Philippians 3:13–15 NLV)

Our calling, our mission, our life is to follow Jesus Christ—to be His sons, servants, princes, leaders, friends, translators, priests, and ambassadors in our world. Represent Him. Make a difference. Give our lives up for His life, as He did His own for us.

Immanuel—God with us—has called your name and wants you to be His friend and confidant to change the world. What higher calling could you possibly be offered? What greater satisfaction in life could there possibly be? What greater love has any man than this?

So will we fall? Yes. Will we fail? Yes. Will we even at times betray Him and each other? Yes. But He knows that and made the way for us through His sacrifice on the cross and shed blood for us. His love is greater than our sin. His grace is greater than our garbage.

Gentlemen, we are not monks in a mission, but men on a mission!

I leave you with Paul's challenge to all Christ's warriors.

And that about wraps it up. God is strong, and he wants you strong. So take everything the Master has set out for you, well-made weapons of the best materials. And put them to use so you will be able to stand up to everything the Devil throws your way. This is no afternoon athletic contest that we'll walk away from and forget about in a couple of hours. This is for keeps, a life-or-death fight to the finish against the Devil and all his angels.

Be prepared. You're up against far more than you can handle on your own. Take all the help you can get, every weapon God has issued, so that when it's all over but the shouting you'll still be on your feet. Truth, righteousness, peace, faith, and salvation are more than words. Learn how to apply them. You'll need them throughout your life. God's Word is an indispensable weapon. In the same way, prayer is essential in this ongoing warfare. Pray hard and long. Pray for your brothers and sisters. Keep your eyes open. Keep each other's spirits up so that no one falls behind or drops out. (Ephesians 6:10–18 MSG)

Your heavenly Father knows you well and wants to help you become all He believes you can be!

Now, go get 'em!

Beginning a Relationship with God Through Jesus Christ

If at any point as you went through this book, you had the question, "So how do I begin a relationship with God?" then first and most important, if at all possible, we recommend you talk to a pastor, priest, or mature Christian regarding this significant spiritual decision.

Here we offer you a simple explanation of the Gospel of Jesus Christ.

There is a God-shaped hole, or emptiness, inside each of us. We all try to fill this void in our own way. We cannot see on our own that God Himself is the answer to our emptiness. His Spirit has to help us.

The Bible defines sin as attitudes, thoughts, and actions that displease God. Every person since Adam and Eve has had this problem. Even if we try really hard to be "good," we still make selfish decisions that are not pleasing to a perfect God.

In Paul's letter to the Roman church, he created a pattern that lays out a path to salvation in Christ. For millions of people, these simple yet profound truths have led to new life.

For ever since the world was created, people have seen the earth and sky. Through everything God made, they can clearly see his invisible qualities—his eternal power and divine nature. So they have no excuse for not knowing God. Yes, they knew God, but they wouldn't worship him as God or even give him thanks. And they began to think up foolish ideas of what God was like. As a result, their minds became dark and confused. (Romans 1:20–21)

We are made right with God by placing our faith in Jesus Christ. And this is true for everyone who believes, no matter who we are. For everyone has sinned; we all fall short of God's glorious standard. Yet God, in his grace, freely makes us right in his sight. He did this through Christ Jesus when he freed us from the penalty for our sins. (Romans 3:22–24)

But God showed his great love for us by sending Christ to die for us while we were still sinners. (Romans 5:8)

For the wages of sin is death, but the free gift of God is eternal life through Christ Jesus our Lord. (Romans 6:23)

If you openly declare that Jesus is Lord and believe in your heart that God raised him from the dead, you will be saved. For it is by believing in your heart that you are made right with God, and it is by openly declaring your faith that you are saved. (Romans 10:9–10)

For "Everyone who calls on the name of the Lord will be saved." (Romans 10:13)

For everything comes from him and exists by his power and is intended for his glory. All glory to him forever! Amen. (Romans 11:36)

Countless people have begun a relationship with God through Jesus Christ after reading Paul's words guiding to salvation. This is the truth of the Gospel. But God gives you the choice. If you are ready to begin a relationship with Christ, there is a strong likelihood that there is someone in your life who would love to know, is ready to talk with you about this important choice, and answer any questions to guide you in your decision. Please talk to someone as soon as you can.

If you know that you are ready to begin a relationship with Christ right now, while there are no magic words or a specific formula for receiving God's gift of salvation, we have included a simple prayer for guidance:

"Dear God, I know I am a sinner and need Your forgiveness. I now turn from my sins and ask You into my life to be my Savior and Lord. I choose to follow You, Jesus. Please forgive my sins and give me Your gift of eternal life. Thank You for dying for me, saving me, and changing my life. In Jesus' name. Amen."

For I am not ashamed of this Good News about Christ. It is the power of God at work, saving everyone who believes—the Jew first and also the Gentile. (Romans 1:16)

Small Group Accountability Questions

Depending on the needs of your group, some of these questions you may want to answer every week, while others you may decide to switch up. Feel free to use what you like. These can also act as a guide to write your own questions to fit your group.

<u>Sword—Offense:</u>

How was your relationship with God?

How was your Bible reading/study?

How was your prayer life?

Did you pray with your wife/family?

How did you grow in your marriage?

How did you grow as a father?

What is one teaching point you gained and grew from?

Where was your strongest place of spiritual growth?

Is there a situation where you gave sacrificially?

How did you see God use you?

What was your greatest blessing?

Shield—Defense:

Was there a moment where you disappointed yourself?

Has any particular temptation or sin been strong in your life?

How have you done in your mind/thoughts?

Have you struggled with a sexual temptation? How have you fought it?

Have you committed any sexual sin?

How has your attitude been?

How has your mouth/speech been?

Did you compromise your integrity?

Was there a situation where you hurt or offended someone?

Was there a situation where you were a taker without regard for the other person?

End Notes

[1] Merriam-Webster Online Dictionary, s.v. "believe," https://www.merriam-webster.com/dictionary/believe.

[2] Merriam-Webster Online Dictionary, s.v. "become," https://www.merriam-webster.com/dictionary/become.

[3] Merriam-Webster Online Dictionary, s.v. "be," https://www.merriam-webster.com/dictionary/be.

[4] Linda Dillow, What's It Like Being Married to Me? (Colorado Springs: David C Cook, 2011), 156

[5] Chris Carrier, "I Faced My Killer Again," Crosswalk, https://www.crosswalk.com/11622274/.

[6] Ellen Banks Elwell, The One Year Devotions for Moms (Carol Stream, IL: Tyndale House, 2005), July 26

[7] Merriam-Webster Online Dictionary, s.v. "ruminate," https://www.merriam-webster.com/dictionary/ruminate.

The Sword & Shield:
A 40-Day Devotional Journey for Men

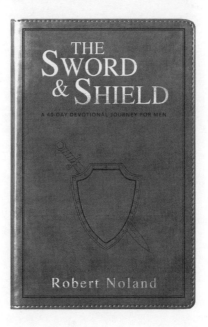

The Sword & Shield 40-Day Devotional Journey for Men is a 40-day journey designed to encourage, inspire, and challenge men to be leaders for Christ in their families, workplaces, and circles of influence.

AVAILABLE AT:

iDisciple   Christianbook   amazon

www.swordandshielddevo.com

The Sword & Shield Podcast

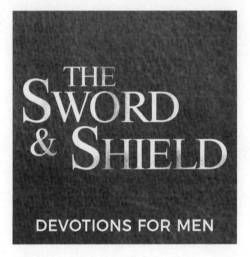

Author and communicator Robert Noland shares stories, analogies, and Bible teaching to spur men on in their spiritual journey of following Jesus.

Available on Apple, Spotify, Google, Breaker, Overcast, Pocket Casts, Podbean, and RadioPublic